Pagan Portals

Seeking the Primal Goddess

The Magic & Mystery of the Hearth Fire

Companion title to *Pan: Dark Lord of the Forest*
and Horned God of the Witches

Pagan Portals

Seeking the Primal Goddess

The Magic & Mystery of the Hearth Fire

Companion title to *Pan: Dark Lord of the Forest*
and Horned God of the Witches

Mélusine Draco

MOON
BOOKS

Winchester, UK
Washington, USA

JOHN HUNT PUBLISHING

First published by Moon Books, 2020
Moon Books is an imprint of John Hunt Publishing Ltd., No. 3 East Street, Alresford
Hampshire SO24 9EE, UK
office@jhpbooks.net
www.johnhuntpublishing.com
www.moon-books.net

For distributor details and how to order please visit the 'Ordering' section on our website.

Text copyright: Mélusine Draco 2019

ISBN: 978 1 78904 256 6
978 1 78904 257 3 (ebook)
Library of Congress Control Number: 2018959640

A CIP catalogue record for this book is available from the British Library.

Design: Stuart Davies

UK: Printed and bound by CPI Group (UK) Ltd, Croydon, CR0 4YY
US: Printed and bound by Thomson-Shore, 7300 West Joy Road, Dexter, MI 48130

We operate a distinctive and ethical publishing philosophy in
all areas of our business, from our global network of authors to
production and worldwide distribution.

Contents

Dedicated to all the members of Coven of the Scales
– past, present and future.

Vocatus atque non vocatus deus aderit
'Called or not called, the god will be present'

Chapter One

Nature, Nurture or Nemesis

Belief is possibly one of the least tangible and yet, at the same time, the most tangible of human faculties. Belief can be rock solid or a crumbling edifice; it can be a deep-rooted family faith or a recently discovered Path with all its mysteries intact. In the 21st century it is no longer a foregone conclusion that many of the current generation will be following the faith and beliefs of their forefathers. In fact, with the exception of the fundamentalist faiths, that which was once inflexible has become extremely flexible indeed.

The advent of social media has advanced the growth of Paganism across the globe and highlighted the fact that millions of people are now identifying with ancient cultures to which they have no obvious racial connection. And although poor old Carl Jung's core concepts of synchronicity, archetypes and the collective subconscious are dismissed as out-dated, they still strongly resonate with those of a magical-mystical persuasion. In fact, one of the earliest criticisms of Jung's work was that it was 'anti-scientific in its intentions as well as its content' - but much the same could be said about magic, which is, in itself often considered to be an amalgam of science and art. Jung's view of the functions of symbolism in dreams led to his isolation from the mainstream psychiatric community, and as he put it, 'My book was declared to be rubbish; I was a mystic, and that settled the matter', since his view of symbolism appeared to undermine the 'scientific' status of psychology.

Yet symbols and sigils *have* long been the language of magic and mysticism, particularly in the realms of divination and esoteric Qabalistic writings. While in *The Power of Images*, David Freedberg, a Professor of Art History at Columbia University, opined some eighty years later that there *has* been a very definite relationship between images and people throughout history. There *were* certain kinds of response – psychological and behavioural – that had appeared to have been observed throughout history and across cultures whether 'civilised' or 'primitive'. According to the Professor they were not usually addressed because they were unrefined, basic, pre-intellectual, raw – and, well ... *primal*:

> They were too embarrassing or awkward to write about. But I kept encountering them, by chance and haphazardly, in a wide variety of ethnographic and historical sources, and they seemed to be constantly and consistently figured in commonplaces and metaphors ... What follows deals with the sort of behaviour that rational positives like to describe as irrational, superstitious, or primitive, only explicable in terms of 'magic'. I would in fact, be happy if the long-standing distinctions between objects that elicit particular responses because of imputed 'religious' or 'magical' powers could be collapsed ... Indeed it seems to me that we should now be prepared to remove the evidence of phenomena like the animism of images from discussions of 'magic', and that we should confront more squarely the extent to which such phenomena tell us about the use and function of images themselves and of the responses to them.

Jung thought of his archetypes as primordial images within the basic structure of the human psyche that have appeared repeatedly in myths, symbols, and personified forms throughout human history. The similarity of the motifs and themes in these myths and symbols of many different cultures suggested the existence of a collective unconscious shared by all human beings. A vaguely similar train of thought to David Freedberg's but Art obviously had no fear of rushing in where Science feared to tread.

Jung's interest in mysticism and occultism has frequently been dismissed by 'rational-minded' scholars as historical curiosities and/or primitive superstitions. Those who believed that the scientific and technological achievements of the West proved the superiority of its culture over all others were understandably offended by Jung's notion that the West's one-sided emphasis on progress needed balance or compensation similar to Eastern modes of thought. Unfortunately, from a scientific point of view, Jung failed to explore how Gnosticism and the Eastern systems functioned within their own specific historical and social contexts, and tended to assign all of them equal value and relevance. Then again, Jung had never been schooled in the various esoteric disciplines ... but neither had his detractors.

In psychology, genetic memory is said to be a memory present at birth that exists in the absence of sensory experience, and is incorporated into the genome over long spans of time. It is based on the idea that common experiences of a species become incorporated into its genetic code with a readiness to respond in certain ways to certain stimuli. According to psychologist Dr. Darold Treffert, genetic memory, simply put, 'refers to complex abilities and actual sophisticated knowledge inherited along with other more typical and commonly accepted physical and behavioural characteristics'. In magical practitioners, however, this esoteric 'chip' comes factory installed and relies on certain external imagery or stimuli to activate it, but once exposed to the mysterious world of symbol and sigil, analogy and metaphor, the recipient instinctively begins to understand its 'hidden' language.

Esoterically speaking, this stimuli can be said to come from our own personal *daemon* or guardian. In the ancient Greek religion, *daemon* designates not a specific class of divine beings, but a peculiar mode of activity: it is an occult power that drives humans forward or acts against them. Hence *daemon* is the veiled countenance of divine activity, a spiritual being who watches over each individual, and is tantamount to a higher self, or guardian angel.

> Daemons scarcely figure in Greek mythology or Greek art:
> they are felt, but their unseen presence can only be presumed,
> with the exception of the *agathodaemon* - personal companion
> spirits comparable to the Roman *genii*, who ensured
> good luck, health, and wisdom – who were honoured first
> with a libation in ceremonial wine-drinking, and represented
> in iconography by the chthonic serpent. In a wider sense,
> from the Roman perspective and perhaps in a mote truly
> animistic sense, the *genius* was the spirit that dwells in man,
> as a spirit that dwelt in the hearth. The symbol of the *genius*
> was the 'house-snake', a sacred inhabitant whose recognition
> goes back into a very primitive past. [*Phases in the Religion of
> Ancient Rome*]

Throughout history, writers and artists of esoteric material
typically (and often annoyingly) use allegories such as these as
literary or visual devices to convey these semi-hidden or complex
meanings. Through the use of symbolic figures, actions, imagery,
or events, these can be interpreted to reveal a hidden moral,
magical or mystical significance not immediately obvious to the
casual onlooker. For example, the serpent, or snake, is one of the
oldest, most widespread and powerful mythological symbols in
the world and has been associated with some of the oldest, most
sacred rituals known to humankind. In some cultures, snakes
were fertility symbols, while in others the creature symbolised
the umbilical cord, joining all humans to Mother Earth, the Great
Mother, or the primal Great Goddess.

> While the snake is possibly the most provocative symbol
> associated with female archetypes, for its suggestive shape
> and its association with death and rebirth, the underworld,
> the supernatural, and the generative powers of nature; other

common forms taken by the anima and mother archetypes are the feline and the bird. With the feline, we depart from the stygian depths of the unconscious or underworld of the mind, and inhabit the terrestrial surface in daylight. Yet, we find that however remote from the unconscious/ underworld these sky goddesses appear to be, many of them have an intimate relationship with the underworld, without which they would not be complete. [*The Archetypal Female in Mythology and Religion: The Anima and the Mother of the Earth and Sky*, Dr. Joan Relke]

The Primal Goddess often had snakes as her familiars - sometimes twining around her sacred staff, as in ancient Crete - where they were worshiped as guardians of her Mysteries of birth and regeneration. This persona in ancient Minoan society was Britomartis, the Cretan goddess of nature, hunters and fishermen; as Mountain Mother and in archaic art she was portrayed with demonic features and shown holding the double-axes of power, together with her symbols - the divine snakes. Worshipped as the Minoan moon-goddess of the mountains in later Mycenaean times and representing the female spirit of nature, Britomartis was the name of the Great Goddess of life, death and resurrection; and was among the Minoan goddess figures that passed through the Mycenaean culture into classical Greek mythology.

The easily recognisable ancient symbol of three conjoined spirals may also have had triple-goddess significance similar to the imagery that lies behind the Greek *triskelion,* (a three-legged symbol dating back to when Sicily was part of Magna Graecia), since the triple spiral motif is a Neolithic symbol in Western Europe. Though popularly considered a 'Celtic' symbol, it is in fact a *pre*-Celtic image, found carved into the rock of a stone lozenge near the main entrance of the prehistoric Newgrange monument in Ireland; which was built around 3200BC and predates the Celtic arrival in Ireland, but has long since been incorporated into Celtic culture.

This labyrinthine symbolism manifests in the sacred spiral – representing the universal pattern of growth and evolution, eternity and continuity; it is also a dynamic symbol in that it represents energy. In fact if we look at pure energy under a microscope we will see that energy forms spiral patterns and is Nature's way of creating and sustaining a recurring pattern to evolve life at every scale. We can see it everywhere – in atoms, cells, seeds, flowers, trees, animals, humans, hurricanes, planets, suns, galaxies and even the cosmos as a whole. It is the same energy we can feel with a magnet. It is usually invisible, but by going back to those early school science lessons and scattering iron filings loosely around a magnet we can actually see the 'shape' of energy. In order for the pattern to show up on every scale, there must be a way for organisms to grow while maintaining proportion among their parts. There is one spiral vortex in Nature that accomplishes this – and it's called the 'phi spiral' and can be seen as everything comes into form, from tiny ferns to giant galaxies – and forms the basis for what has come to be known as 'sacred geometry'.

This sacred geometry also ascribes symbolic and sacred meanings to certain geometric shapes and certain geometric proportions, and is associated with the belief that a god/creator is the geometer of the world. This is the geometry used in the design and construction of religious structures such as temples, cathedrals, ancient monuments and altars, while the concept also applies to sacred spaces such as *temenoi* (a sacred enclosure), sacred groves, and holy wells, and, as far as the Primal Goddess is concerned, the creation of religious art in Old Europe.

Nevertheless, the belief that a 'god' created the universe according to a geometric plan has ancient origins. Plutarch attributed the belief to Plato, writing that 'Plato said god geometrizes continually' (*Convivialium disputationum*, liber 8,2). Geometric ratios and geometric figures were often employed in the architectural designs of ancient Egypt, India, Greece and Rome; medieval European cathedrals also incorporated symbolic geometry with the most impressive being the labyrinth on the floor of Chartres Cathedral in France. Many of the sacred geometric principles of the human body and of ancient architecture were compiled into the 'Vitruvian Man' drawing by Leonardo da Vinci, the drawing itself based on the much older writings of the Roman architect Vitruvius.

Similarly, the circle is also ancient and universal - it represents the infinite nature of energy and symbolises the universe. It has been used as a symbol since the beginning of time and ancient cultures all over the world used the image to represent the same thing: unity, infinity - as well as sacredness, the goddess, female power, and, conversely - the sun. To earth-centered religions throughout history, as well as for contemporary Paganism, it represents the feminine spirit or force, the cosmos or a spiritualised Mother Earth, and, of course, the sacred space or Compass.

The circle is a profound, transcendent symbol. It is said to represent wholeness, completion, inclusion, the life cycle, heaven, eternity, and the universe. Yet circles are not just symbolic: they are a natural physical phenomena, too. When scientists look at the building blocks of humankind - our DNA - they find spirals or stacked interlocking circles. Indeed, in the whorls of our fingertips, the irises of our eyes, our cells and the egg that gave each of us life, we are made of circles. And we live on a circular planet that receives the light of our circular life-giving sun - our survival depends on circles.

See how quickly we have moved on from the snake goddess symbolism of the ancient world to cutting-edge science of the 21st century? Nevertheless, there can be no denying the fact that these signs and symbols *are* an integral part of an inherited magical power that has an unbroken link with the ancient world.

Two simple symbols – the spiral and the circle.

The Nature vs Nurture debate also enters the equation as to what extent particular aspects of our behaviour are a product of either inherited (i.e. genetic) or acquired (i.e. learned) characteristics. Nature is what we can think of as our 'pre-wiring' and is influenced by genetic inheritance and other biological factors; nurture is generally taken as the influence of external factors after conception e.g. the product of exposure, experience and learning on an individual. Again, that factory-installed esoteric 'chip' is merely waiting on certain external imagery or stimuli to activate it in the so-called Elect.

This cognisance, however, is often the mystic or magical practitioner's Nemesis - the inescapable agent of his or her downfall – since its inheritance has always been considered both blessing and curse. In the ancient Greek religion, Nemesis was the goddess who enacted retribution against those who succumb to hubris (or arrogance before the gods) and those who pursue magical knowledge as a power-tool can still find themselves headed for DIY destruction. This 'magic' gene can lie dormant for generations but *will* eventually surface in some unsuspecting soul, who immediately understands that there will be a price to pay for its largess, no matter how hard they try or ignore or dismiss the often unwelcome gift.

What if, for example, the realisation that the Great Mother of contemporary paganism bears no similarity to the primal Great Goddess of the Old European world? For in truth, the original gods and goddesses of ancient times were monstrous beings – often slain by their own more comely off-spring to create a Classic *Game of Thrones*–type saga of the emerging civilisations, such as the vanquishing of the Great Mother of the Mesopotamian myth – Tiamat, the primeval dragon-like monster of original chaos. These Creators have been seen as both male *and* female, wonderful and awesome, terrible and unknowable – they are usually the oldest beings in any pantheon on earth and certainly not in any comely human form as portrayed by the Pre-Raphaelite movement!

Even Gaia, the universal Earth Mother, has her monstrous side in spawning a whole host of dysfunctional off-spring. As one of the Greek primordial deities, she is the ancestral mother of all life: seen as the primal Mother-Earth goddess. Hesiod's *Theogony* tells how, after Chaos, 'wide-bosomed' Gaia (Earth) arose to be the everlasting seat of the immortals who possess Olympus above, and the depths of Tartarus below. He then tells that Gaia brought forth her equal Uranus (Heaven-Sky) to 'cover her on every side' and to be the abode of the gods. Gaia also bore the hills (*ourea*), and Pontus (Sea), 'without sweet union of love' (i.e., with no father).

Afterwards with Uranus she gave birth to the Titans, and as Hesiod tells it: '*She lay with Heaven* and bore deep-swirling *Oceanus, Coeus, and Crius and Hyperion and Iapetus, Theia and Rhea, Themis and Mnemosyne and gold-crowned Phoebe and lovely Tethys. After them was born Kronos the wily, youngest and most terrible of her children, and he hated his lusty sire*'. Benefitting from Gaia's advice, Zeus, her grandson, defeated the Titans, but afterwards, Gaia, in union with Tartarus, bore the youngest of her sons, the monstrous, serpentine Typhon, who would be the last challenger to the authority of Zeus.

Some modern academic sources claim that Gaia as 'Mother Earth' is a later form of a pre-Indo-European Great Mother, venerated in Neolithic times – or Old Europe - although others assign the mother-goddess Cybele from Anatolia as being identified by the Greeks with Gaia. The mythological name was revived in 1979 by James Lovelock, in *Gaia: A New Look at Life on Earth*. His Gaia Hypothesis, which proposes that living organisms and inorganic material are part of a dynamical system that shapes the Earth's biosphere, maintains the Earth as a fit environment for life. In some Gaia-theories, the Earth itself is viewed as an organism with self-regulatory functions.

Further books by Lovelock and others popularised the Gaia Hypothesis, which was embraced to some extent by New Age environmentalists as part of the heightened awareness of environmental concerns of the 1990s. As a result, many pagans worship Gaia with beliefs ranging from her being viewed as the Earth itself, to the belief that she is the spiritual embodiment of the Earth, or as the Goddess of the Earth – very few actually visualise her as the primal goddess of Old Europe.

It is often said that humankind created the gods in their own image and art has always been at the forefront of how we interpret the appearance of our deities. From the exquisite interpretation of a statue executed in marble some 5,000-years ago, this sculpture of a female figure is commonly known as 'Stargazer' because her eyes are looking upwards to the stars. Similar to later Cycladic art that flourished in the islands of the Aegean, this ancient masterpiece is of the Kilia-type from Anatolia, created in translucent marble, and it a very rare piece indeed. The head is sculpted entirely in the round, while the body is reduced to a simple yet elegant profile; the nose is depicted as a slight ridge on a straight-line edge with the head tilted backwards, the eyes are tiny dots raised in relief. Created in the early Bronze Age, the purpose of this masterpiece is unknown but as the Cleveland Museum of Art says: "All we can do is speculate on the creative and spiritual forces that created this beautiful and mystical figure that symbolises our search for the divine."

Similarly, in the early days of Egyptian antiquity, and roughly within the same time-frame as the Stargazer, many of the gods were abstract concepts rather than actual 'god pictures' and many of the later deities were merely theological concepts represented by a distinctive hieroglyph. As the need for visualisation grew, so did the spiritual need for more tangible forms on which to focus the people's devotions. The common human mind dwelt on the concrete, not the abstract and so the gods took on animal-human shape to satisfy the religious-teaching-by-pictures demands of less scholarly folk. The attributes of the major gods subsequently extended to create a whole pantheon of relatives and helpers. For example, the concept of *ma'at* as the symbolic terminology for cosmic order and earthly truth and justice was depicted in the *Pyramid Texts* by an ostrich feather. This concept later metamorphosed into a beautiful woman, who sat in judgement - she was sometimes shown as the wife of Thoth, or the female embodiment of the god.

Following this 'anthropomorphic evolution' the individual deities were distinguished and immediately identifiable by their different head-dresses and by various attributes inherited from the original primitive animal-forms, which in many cases, still surmount their heads. Historian, Paul Hamlyn writes that the divine types seem to be fixed as far as artistic representation is concerned, from Dynasty II. "Thus art provides an element of continuity throughout three millennia, whatever the significance attributed to the gods at different periods may have been."

Many of these regionalised deities survived and found their way into the vast pictorial wealth of Egyptian temple carving; while the images created by ancient craftsmen to be placed in tombs, or used as votive statues for temples, were 'considered essential for the welfare of the individual in death as in life'. Very few of these statues from the early dynasties were ever intended to be viewed by mortal men, since they were destined to be hidden from sight forever once the tomb had been sealed, or they had been placed in the inner-most sanctuary of the funerary temple. [*Liber Ægyptius*]

T G H James, former Assistant Keeper in the Department of Egyptian Antiquities at the British Museum, made a very valid point in that very little archaic sculpture was ever made which did not have a specific function quite independent of art. From the colossal statues to the tiny funerary figures, each piece was created as a religious (in its widest sense) image as opposed to having any decorative function. Every relief or carving depicted the deity, king or noble in a manner that ensured a continuance of 'life' in the Otherworld and so each form had to obey the 'cannons of form and proportion' that governed all Egyptian art. The appreciation of the Egyptian approach to art is often a question of personal taste, since many of the general criticisms often levelled at the style is that the images are 'stiff, unfeeling, angular, hieratic, cold, without spirit'. For others, the sheer physical beauty, the divine spark of serenity and spirituality, the strength and power of the subject overshadow any 'strangenesses' in perspective.

The ancient Greeks, by contrast, were masters of physical perfection when it came to creating images of their deities. In fact, classic Greek art stands out among that of other cultures for its development of naturalistic but idealized depictions of the human body, in which largely nude male figures were generally the focus of innovation. Ancient Greek monumental sculpture was composed almost entirely of marble or bronze; with cast bronze becoming the favoured medium for major works by the early 5th century; many pieces of sculpture now known only in marble copies made for the Roman market were originally made in bronze. Smaller works were in a great variety of materials, many of them precious, with a very large production of terracotta figurines.

The Greeks also decided very early on that the human form was the most important subject for artistic endeavour. Seeing their gods as having human form, there was no distinction between the sacred and the secular in art - the human body *was* both secular and sacred. A male nude without any attachments such as a bow or a club could just as easily be Apollo or Heracles as that year's Olympic boxing champion! Statues such as the *Apollo Belvedere* (or *Pythian Apollo*) was considered the greatest ancient sculpture by ardent neo-classicists, and for centuries epitomized ideals of aesthetic perfection for Europeans and westernised parts of the world.

Praxiteles's Knidian Aphrodite, however, revolutionized Greek statuary. Previous sculptures showed women clothed without exception, and while a number of artists used the 'wet drapery' effect to display women's bodies in an acceptable manner none had made the leap to establishing a female nude. Praxiteles's method of bridging the gap and depicting an unclothed woman - without causing too much of an outrage - was considered inspired. By choosing Aphrodite, the goddess of love and sexuality, as his subject, he had found a way to justify female nudity. By toeing the line between sensual and modest, dignified yet welcoming, Praxiteles depicted the nude in a way considered inoffensive by his audience.

Contemporary depictions of 'the goddess' in pagan art, however, owe more to the influence of the pre-Raphaelite Brotherhood and the Aesthetic Movement. Not to mention **Lawrence Alma-Tadema**, a classical-subject painter, who became famous for his depictions of the luxury and decadence of the Roman Empire, with languorous figures set in fabulous marbled interiors, or against a dazzling blue Mediterranean backdrop of sea and sky. But as modern artist Jason Pitzl-Waters observes: "One of the most obvious legacies our modern world holds from its pre-Christian 'pagan' past are the visual arts. There wouldn't have been a Renaissance without the art and writings of the Classical world, and the pagan-humanist hybrid that began there has been an integral part of the fine arts ever since."

However we view 'deity', of course, is entirely dependent on an individual's perception – 'the identification, and interpretation of sensory information in order to represent and understand the presented information, or the environment', according to David Freedberg's *The Power of Images*. Our perception is not only the unconscious receipt of these signals, but it's also shaped by our learning, memory, expectation, and attention. In the case of visual perception, some people can actually see the percept shift in their mind's eye, while other who are not 'picture thinkers', may not necessarily perceive the 'shape-shifting' as their world changes. Perception also depends on complex functions of the nervous system, but subjectively seems mostly effortless because this processing happens outside our conscious awareness, if we accept Jung's viewpoint. Because of the way they've been schooled in the art of witchcraft, Old Craft witches are more likely to 'see' their goddess figure in terms of the Stargazer; while contemporary Paganism appears to favour the predominantly medievalist forms of Burne-Jones and Rossetti. And perceptions *do* change. When archaeologist, Margaret Murray, wrote her ground-breaking God of the Witches in 1931, fellow academics quickly dismissed her theory of a universal, pre-Christian cult of witches who worshiped a singular mother goddess as nonsense. However, she wasn't so completely off-base as later archaeologists like Marija Gimbutas, have revealed. Many early societies *did* have a mother-like god-form, and honoured the sacred feminine with their ritual, art and legends. Take, for instance, the ancient carvings of rounded, curved, feminine forms found in Willendorf. These 'Venus' figurines - a term given to a collection of prehistoric statuettes of women made during the Palaeolithic Period – are mostly found in Europe, but with finds as far away as Siberia.

To date, more than 200 of them have been found, all of whom are portrayed with similar physical attributes, including curvaceous bodies with large breasts, bottoms, abdomen, hips, and thighs, and usually tapered at the top and bottom. The heads are often of relatively small and devoid of detail; most are missing hands and feet. Some appear to represent pregnant women, while others show no such signs. The figurines were carved from all manner of different materials, ranging from soft stone (such as steatite, calcite, or limestone) to bone, ivory, or clay. The oldest statuette so far discovered was uncovered in 2008 in Germany - the Venus of Hohle Fels as the figure has been called - was carved from a mammoth's tusk that dates to at least 35,000 years old.

These icons are the symbol of something once revered by pre-Christian cultures in Europe, like the Norse and Roman societies, who honored the deities of women within their shrines and temples. According to Dr. Relke, this mother-goddess archetype expresses itself culturally and personally in the roles of various mother goddesses and spiritual figures, often conflating into one mythological character. *The Archetypal Female in Mythology and Religion: The Anima and the Mother of the Earth and Sky* divides these archetypes into three realms, each with its own characteristics: underworld, earth, and sky. She discussed the anima and the mother archetypes as they manifest as underworld figures, concerned primarily with the non-rational forces of the unconscious – supernatural knowledge, sexuality, the enthralling mother - and the anima's personification of the 'chaotic urge to life'. These underworld figures often take the forms of snakes or serpents and fish or sea creatures:

> Contemporary paganism emphasises the Great Goddess in her benevolent, nurturing, caring aspect, and would no doubt see in Jung's attitude a reflection of the patriarchal fear of the feminine, which they claim prevailed as prehistoric matristic cultures succumbed to the authoritarian, war-like patriarchal cultures of the historic ancient world, doing a great disservice in recasting the goddesses in a negative light. Politics aside, the mother archetype in myth does display an ambivalent or dual nature. Demeter rages, cursing the earth with drought until Persephone is released. Kali drips with the blood of her devoured children. Gaia, through her son, castrates her spouse; the priests of Cybele castrate themselves in a religious frenzy; Isis curses and nearly kills the great god

Re; the Sphinx strangles Thebes. The Great Mother delivers and cares for us all, even though in the end, she destroys and subsumes us into her 'thrall'.

But what if there *was* a 'magico-spiritual' gene that could be traced back to those distant ancestors who actually worshipped the forebears of the various deities to whom we claim allegiance today? If all the massive movements of people in Continental Europe happened some 10,000 years ago following the last receding Ice Age, to which gods did they pay homage for those remaining 8,000-years before monotheism had large numbers of the Earth's population marching to the same (or a similar) drum? Because there *are* time-honoured things about us all as *individuals* that are bred deep in the bone; we are what our roots (DNA) claim us to be. We cannot escape those ancient racial memories of where we came from even if the descendants of yesterday's pagans are now scattered all over the globe. Our personal daemon lurks with us in the amniotic fluid we float in before our birth; or as some believe from the moment of conception.

So ... at what stage in our genetic memory is that factory-installed esoteric 'chip' ready to be activated by those 'complex abilities and the actual sophisticated knowledge', inherited along with other more typical and commonly accepted physical and behavioural characteristics'? What gives us that insight into the mind of Neith, an early, pre-dynastic goddess in the Egyptian pantheon, said to be the first and the prime Creatrix of the universe and all it contains, and who governs how it functions: '*I am the things that are, that will be, and that have been...*' What causes us to suddenly 'log-on' to that collective subconscious and become imbued with such a certainty that we can say to ourselves - "*I don't need to believe, I know!*"

The Hearth Fire: Exercise 1.
The fundamental teaching of traditional British Old Craft is

that the 'Creator' is everything, physical and non-physical, literally everything and therefore incomprehensible to our finite understanding. Being everything, the Creator *is male and female and androgyne*. All things are created in the image of the Creator, because the Creator is every part of everything. The Creator has no specific regard or concern for one species - i.e. humankind - among millions of species on one insignificant minor planet, in an outer arm of a spiral galaxy, which is one among millions...

Those coming new to Old Craft teaching often have a problem in coming to terms with 'deity' being viewed in the abstract and one of the best ways of combating this is to introduce them to representations of ancient Cycladic and Kilia-type figurines. The majority of these figures are highly stylized representations of the female human form, typically having a flat, geometric quality which gives them a striking resemblance to today's modern art. According to archaeologist Marija Gimbutas, who has considered these artefacts from an anthropological viewpoint, believes they are 'representative of a Great Goddess of nature in a tradition continuous with that of Neolithic female figures such as the Venus of Willendorf'.

Although the Kilia type statuettes are considerably earlier in date (4500-3500BC) than related figures produced in the Cyclades, they are probably also linked with that ancient fertility and eternal life cycle, a central spiritual concern in the ancient Mediterranean. I had hoped to use the 'Stargazer' on the front cover of *Seeking the Primal Goddess* but the Cleveland Museum of Art wanted to charge such an exorbitant fee that it had to be something else. Nevertheless, the Stargazer is a good place to start since she is the perfect symbol for representing Underworld, Earth and Sky, which are the domains of the Old European Goddess and yet has a decidedly modern feel about her semi-androgynous image.

- **Obtain a replica image or picture book featuring these** images and meditate on the ancient forms of the Primal Goddess while sitting by the hearth fire. Down-load a copy of the Stargazer and her ancient companions, together with a couple of the academic papers listed in the Source and Bibliography at the end of the book. Here, in the light of the flickering flames we are preparing ourselves for thinking in abstract forms when it comes to visualising the 'Owd Lass' of Old Craft belief - where we use primitive ideas over the more romantic concept of contemporary Paganism.

Chapter Two

Spiritual Bloodline

What have archaeologists, Professors Barry Cunliffe and Marija Gimbutas, and geneticist, Professor Bryan Sykes got in common, besides being highly respected scientists within their own fields of research? Answer: Their researches chronicle the mass migrations of people and culture throughout ancient Europe.

According to Marija Gimbutas, matrilineality is the tracing of descent through the female line. It may also correlate with a societal system in which each person is identified with their matriline – their mother's lineage – and which can involve the inheritance of property and/or titles. A matriline is a line of descent from a female ancestor to a descendant (of either sex) in which the individuals in all intervening generations are mothers – in other words, a 'mother line'. In a matrilineal descent system, an individual is considered to belong to the same descent group as her or his mother. This matrilineal descent pattern is in contrast to the more common pattern of patrilineal descent from which a family name is usually derived.

Bryan Sykes 'studied a tiny percentage of human DNA known as mitochondrial DNA, which unlike most of our genes does not get jumbled up between mother and father from generation to generation. Mitochondrial DNA (mDNA) is passed on unchanged from mother to child, time after time, over thousands - in fact, millions - of years. This extraordinary property means that we do, indeed, carry within us a piece of information passed on directly from a maternal ancestor who lived in the world while the Ice Age was at its height. By comparing mutations in mDNA, which occur spontaneously every 10 millennia or so, it is possible to draw conclusions about the movements of large groups of people over time. It is also possible to identify 'clusters' of present-day people with similar sets of mutations, which can be traced back to putative single maternal ancestors in the distant past' ... [*The Guardian*]

Barry Cunliffe has charted the movement of ancient coastal communities living along the Atlantic seaways during the first millennium BC and the first millennium AD. His researches convinced him that the people of the long Atlantic coastline have shared common beliefs and values over thousands of years conditioned by their unique habitat. They lived in a resource-rich zone, in many ways remote from neighbours by land yet easily linked to others by sea. In *Facing the Ocean*, we can also explore almost 10,000 years of human life from the Mesolithic hunter-gathers to the later explorers who journeyed to lands beyond the horizon after the last Ice Age, and from whom many of us can trace our ancestry.

Surprisingly enough, in the late 19th century, almost all pre-historians and anthropologists following the theory outlined in Lewis H. Morgan's influential book *Ancient Society*, believed that early human kinship was everywhere matrilineal. This idea was also taken up by Friedrich Engels in *The Origin of the Family, Private Property and the State*. The Morgan-Engels thesis stated that humanity's earliest domestic institution was not the family but the matrilineal clan, although most 20th century social anthropologists considered the theory of matrilineal priority untenable. Nevertheless, during the 1970s and 1980s, a range of feminist scholars often attempted to revive the concept and continued to muddy the spiritual waters of our matrilineal and patrilineal descent.

Certain ancient myths have been used to expose ancient traces of matrilineal customs that existed before historical records. The godfather of ancient history, Herodotus, is cited by Robert Graves in his translations of Greek myths as attesting that the Lycians of that time 'still reckoned by matrilineal descent, or were matrilineal, as were the Carians' - from a region of western Anatolia. They were described by Herodotus as being of Minoan Greek descent, while the Carians themselves maintained that they were Anatolian mainlanders intensely engaged in seafaring and were akin to the Mysians and the Lydians.

In Greek (and Egyptian) mythology, while the royal function was a male privilege, power devolution often came through women, and the future king inherited power through marrying the queen-heiress. This is illustrated in the Homeric myths where all the noblest men in Greece vied for the hand of Helen (and the throne of Sparta), as well as the Oedipian cycle where Oedipus, in marrying the recently widowed queen at the same time assumes the Theban kingship. This trend also is evident in many Celtic myths, such as the (Welsh) *Mabinogi* stories of Culhwch and Olwen, or the (Irish) Ulster Cycle, most notably the key facts to the Cúchulainn story that Cúchulainn gets his final secret training with a warrior woman, Scáthach, and becomes the lover of her daughter; and the root of the *Táin Bó Cuailnge,* that while Ailill may wear the crown of Connacht, it is his wife Medb who is the real power, and she needs to affirm her equality to her husband by owning chattels as great as he does.

In the *Iconography and Social Structure of Old Europe* paper presented at the Second Congress on Matrilineal Studies, Joan Marler cited the archaeo-mythological research of Marija Gimbutas, who was hailed as a pioneer in the study of the symbolic imagery of the earliest farming peoples of Europe. Her primary research and interpretations of European prehistory had been at the centre of the most crucial debates on European genesis for more than four decades. In her view, the settlement patterns, burial evidence, and iconographic imagery of the cultures she called 'Old Europe' reflect peaceful, matrilineal, endogamous social structures that were economically egalitarian in which women were honoured at the centre of ceremonial life.

According to Gimbutas, settlement and cemetery evidence as

well as linguistic, mythological and historical research indicate that non-Indo-European Neolithic societies were matrilineal, matrifocal and economically egalitarian. She rejected the term 'matriarchy' because she felt it too often implies a hierarchical structure of domination in which women rule society by force. She made this important observation:

> ... we do not find in Old Europe, nor in all of the Old World, a system of autocratic rule of women with an equivalent suppression of men. Rather, we find a structure in which the sexes are more or less on equal footing, a society that could be termed a gylany [in which] the sexes are linked rather than hierarchically 'ranked'. I use the term 'matristic' simply to avoid the term matriarchy, with the understanding that it incorporates matriliny.

She goes on to say that the prevalence of female-centred cosmological imagery and rituals, and the absence of signs of male dominance support the interpretation of a mother-kinship system in which mothers and grandmothers were honoured and a female ancestor was venerated as progenitor of the lineage.

> The continuity of women's traditions at the centre of cultural life promoted the longevity and cohesion of Old European societies. The spiritual and social worlds were intimately intertwined. Caches of female figures found within ritual contexts ... may reflect councils of women who functioned as collective entities to guide community life.

Not unexpectedly, Professor Gimbutas's theories have been dismissed by many of her fellow archaeologists but like Carl Jung and Margaret Murray, whose work suffered similar professional scorn, there are elements that 'speak' to us on a more subliminal level. As Allen Bennett once observed it's that moment in reading when you come across something ... 'a thought, a feeling, a way of looking at things – which you thought special and particular to you. Now here it is, set down by someone else, a person you have never met, someone even who is long dead. And it is as if a hand has come out and taken yours.' It was as if, in discovering the writings of Marija Gimbutas, the worlds of archaeo-mythologica (Old Europe) and esoteria (Old Craft) collided – and made complete sense of the way we viewed the Primal Goddess within our own Tradition.

We also found ourselves asking, but where exactly was this 'Old European' culture located? In the *Goddesses & Gods of Old Europe*, this area is designated as extending from the Aegean and Adriatic, including the islands of Sicily and Crete, as far north as Czechoslovakia, southern Poland, the western Ukraine and parts of Anatolia.

> Between c7000 and c3500BC the inhabitants of this region developed a much more complex social organisation than their western and northern neighbours, forming settlements which often amounted to small townships, inevitably involving craft specialisation and the creation of religious and governmental institutions ... If one defines civilisation as the ability of a given people to adjust to its environment and to develop adequate arts, technology, script, and social relationships it is evident that Old Europe achieved a marked degree of success.

In *The Language of the Goddess*, we find a major tenant of Gimbutas's theory is that the deeply rooted Old European cultural tradition was *not* responsible for the later patriarchal system that spread across Europe. Instead, this dramatic transformation in the Neolithic social structure, economy, language, and religious beliefs that emerged during the fourth and third millennia BC was not the result of an internal insurgence but a progressive collision between two entirely different ideologies and social systems. Matrilineal society appears based on collective food production but as a highly developed hunting culture gave control of food production to men, so the European societies suppressed a matrilineal influence. And once firmly entrenched, patriarchal rules permeated all spheres of social and cultural life, including religion – and these patriarchal systems continue to this present day.

Bringing together archaeological evidence, comparative mythology and folklore, and symbolic interpretations, Marija Gimbutas's work spotlights the existence in prehistoric Europe of this widespread culture centred on the 'goddess' as life-giver and sustainer, as well as death-wielder. Throughout years of the 'examination of hundreds of Palaeolithic and mostly Neolithic pieces, she systematically traced cross-cultural and cross-chronological symbolic parallels', revealing that the 'central and venerated position of women in the unconscious of early European people seems probable' but this order of things changed with the incursions by groups of Indo-European origin (c.4300-2800BC) as the Old European culture moved from matrilineal to patrilineal.

During the late 1960s, the Blood Transfusion Service's data was examined and a detailed report on the survey of blood groups added to the story of the peopling of Britain. As we all know, human blood is classified according to its constituents into groups A, O, B and AB. Most individuals belong to the groups O or A although those with group O blood exceed those with A blood nearly everywhere in Scotland, Northern Island and most of Wales. Group O blood is present in considerable numbers of people, especially where history hints at survivals of Romano-British life. According to *A Natural History of Man in Britain*:

> The large cities, with the partial exception of Bristol, 'have a marked preponderance of O blood; they have attracted large numbers of landless rural folk rather than the yeoman

farmers of the surrounding countryside. The high percentage of O blood in Ireland and most of Wales, northern England and western Scotland may be thought of in connection with the immigration along the Atlantic route of Neolithic farmers before and after 3000BC. It is generally thought that these early immigrants included many families from Mediterranean lands which have a preponderance of O blood, though there is some B blood in the east of the region.

Pembrokeshire [Where my paternal line comes from, MD], has a relatively high percentage of A blood, accompanied by as much as eighteen percent of B blood. Pembrokeshire, which is often called Little England beyond Wales, had been considerably influenced by Anglo-Norman contacts, and also received numbers of medieval Flemish settlers.

In England there are also high proportions of A blood. They may exceed the percentages with O blood in places which were settled by Anglo-Saxon, Danes and Vikings, viz. east Yorkshire, Lincolnshire, Norfolk, south-east Essex, Kent and east Sussex. North of the Tees and the Ribble the percentage of A blood diminishes rapidly. The Anglo-Saxons came from a region of north-west Germany which has, and also certainly had, a fairly high percentage of A blood; they were essentially rural, took possession of the soil and became a farming population. They displaced the Romano-British elements or converted them into landless serfs; it was the Anglo-Saxons who became the dominant element in the population. [*A Natural History of Man in Britain*]

It's now a well-known fact that that the transfer of mitochondrial DNA from mother to offspring, often called maternal inheritance, is what allows genetic testing services to trace our maternal ancestries because we inherited our mitochondrial DNA from our mother, who inherited hers from her mother and so forth. Both men and women possess mDNA, but only women pass it on to their children. Therefore, mDNA traces an unbroken maternal line back through time for generation upon generation - further back than any written record. In *Blood of the Isles*, Professor Bryan Sykes examined British genetic 'clans' and presented evidence collected from mitochondrial DNA, to make the following surprising points:

- The genetic makeup of Britain and Ireland is overwhelmingly what it has been since the Neolithic period and to a very considerable extent since the Mesolithic period, especially in the female line, i.e. those people, who in time would become identified as British Celts (culturally speaking), but who (genetically speaking) should more properly be called Cro-Magnon.
- The contribution of the Celts of Central Europe to the genetic makeup of Britain and Ireland was minimal; most of the genetic contribution to the British Isles of those we think of as Celtic, came from western continental Europe, i.e. the Atlantic seaboard as shown in great detail by Professor Brian Cunliffe in *Facing the Ocean*.
- The Picts were not a separate people: the genetic makeup of the formerly Pictish areas of Scotland shows no significant differences from the general profile of the rest of Britain. The two 'Pictland' regions are Tayside and Grampian.
- The Anglo-Saxons are supposed to have made a substantial contribution to the genetic makeup of England, but was found to be under twenty percent of the total, even in southern England.
- The Vikings (Danes and Norwegians) have made a substantial contribution, which is concentrated in central, northern and eastern England - the territories of the ancient Danelaw. There is a very heavy Viking contribution in the Orkney and Shetland Islands, in the vicinity of forty

percent. Women as well as men contributed substantially in all these areas, showing that the Vikings engaged in large-scale settlement.

- The Norman contribution was extremely small, in the order of two percent.
- There are only sparse traces of the Roman occupation, almost all in southern England.
- In spite of all these later contributions, the genetic makeup of the British Isles remains overwhelmingly what it was in the Neolithic: a mixture of the first Mesolithic inhabitants with Neolithic settlers who came by sea from Iberia and from the eastern Mediterranean.
- There is a difference between the genetic histories of men and women in Britain and Ireland. The matrilineages show a mixture of original Mesolithic inhabitants and later Neolithic arrivals from Iberia, whereas the patrilineages are much more strongly correlated with Iberia. This suggests replacement of much of the original male population by new arrivals with a more powerful social organization.

A long time before these migratory happenings, however, there was a migration of a different kind – caused by the Ice Age. Herds of migrating game moved away from the worsening conditions and the scattered groups of humans who depended on them for food had no choice but to follow. By the time of the coldest phase of the last Ice Age around 18,000 years ago there were no humans left in Britain, or anywhere else in Europe north of the Alps. The descendants of those nomadic hunters had retreated to southern France, Italy and Spain, abandoning northern Europe to the frost and ice. All evidence of human occupation in northern Britain was obliterated by the ice sheet.

Then the ice began to melt and our ancestors followed the herds north once again, not to mention a large-scale movement along the Atlantic seaboard north from Iberia. The DNA indicates that this was a family-based migration rather than the male-led invasions of later millennia. As Professor Sykes explained:

> After that, the genetic bedrock on the maternal side was in place. By about 6,000 years ago, the pattern was set for the rest of history of the [British] Isles and very little has disturbed it since. Once here the matrilineal DNA mutated and diversified, each region developing slightly different local versions, but without losing its ancient structure.

One of the most significant finds in Britain was the discovery of the Cro-Magnon skeleton of the Red Lady of Paviland Cave on the Gower Peninsula, which dates from the Early Palaeolithic period, some 3,000 years *before* the end of the last Ice Age. First discovered in 1822, the skeleton was thought to be that of a woman, but modern re-examination reveals it to be that of a young man aged 25 to 30. The grave goods included a mammoth ivory bracelet and a perforated periwinkle pendant, numerous seashells and some 50 broken ivory rods. Marker stones were placed at the head and foot of the grave, although the skull was missing.

The DNA extracted from the bones can be related to the commonest ancestry extant in Europe, and strongly suggests that many of our forebears were already inhabiting these islands in the Palaeolithic period, while radio-carbon dating also revealed that some of the artifacts were 'slightly later' than the 'Red Lad's' original burial, indicating that the cave was used repeatedly over a period of some 4,000 years. Without stretching credulity too far, we can surmise that Paviland was a sacred site, and that the Red Lad's burial confirms a significant belief in an afterlife; possibly a form of ancestor worship as is suggested in the careful preservation of the body, and the placement of later offerings. This obviously 'holy man' belonged to the first or earlier part of the Upper Palaeolithic period – just prior to the onset of the last Ice Age that effectively sealed the Red Lad in his ice tomb.

As with all aspects of human evolution, however, nothing is what it seems - and there will always appear be a missing link. But now we've got the general historical stuff out of the way, it's time to carry out a search for the primal goddess of Old Europe and the 'Owd Lass' of traditional witchcraft.

The Hearth Fire: Exercise 2

The Dame of the Coven of the Scales submitted her DNA to Oxford Ancestors for analysis and discovered that she belonged to the Clan of Bryan Sykes's 'Helena', whose origins were firmly rooted in south-western France and the Iberian Peninsula. These were probably the people whose ancestors had created the famous Lascaux cave paintings in the Vézère valley in the Dordogne, and it is here that the first skeletons of Cro-Magnon man were found. The drawings are the combined effort of many generations, and with continued debate, the age of the paintings is estimated at around 17,000 years.

In addition, the Magdalenian and Basque cultures also seem to show remnants of 'Old European' imagery, such as evidence of the triple-goddess at Roc-aux-Sorciers at Vienne in south-eastern France. The name with its suggestion of 'pagan rendezvous', was applied to the site long before the various different artefacts were discovered, among them wall-friezes, the headless and footless figures of women, of the conventionally Venus-type and the relief of 'three colossal female presences with exposed vulvas' – an Old European image that re-emerges in medieval Europe as *sheela-na-gigs*.

Similarly, Mari is still the most important deity in the Basque mythology as a female personification of the earth and a vestige of the earth-based myths worshipped by the matriarchal communities. It is said that Mari was already worshipped as a goddess by the ancient Basque before the arrival of Christianity and taking her attributes into account it is not impossible that she could also be linked to the Goddess of Old European mythology – as can the Morrigan and Brigit of Irish culture.

It is not always possible to distinguish the traces of the Old Ways because over millennia they have become transformed and distorted – and yet it is surprising how long those old concepts have persisted. Or as Professor Gimbutas observes: "The Old European creations were not lost; transformed, they enormously enriched the European psyche ... vestiges of the myth and artistic concepts of Old Europe were transmitted to the modern Western world and became part of its cultural heritage."

- **For this exercise we are looking at a research project into Old Europe's history – not the popular paganism of modern times – so go to the library or go on-line and look up some of the key-words in Exercise 2. See where it leads you as part of a mind-mapping journey and, if you wish, extend it by tracing your own mDNA through the services of Oxford Ancestors or Ancestry.com**

Chapter Three

The Hearth Fire & the Sacred Flame

Despite all this ancestral moving around, it was unavoidable that the incoming Indo-European deities would be amalgamated with the Old European ones, and in the process the much older Goddess lost much of her true identity. According to Professor Gimbutas, the goddesses inherited from Old Europe such as Greek Athene, Hera, Artemis and Hecate; Roman Minerva and Diana; Anatolian Cybele; Irish Morrigan and Brigit; Minoan Britomartis; Baltic Laina and Ragana; Russian Baba Yaga, Basque Mari, and others 'are not 'Venuses' bringing fertility and prosperity – as we shall see, they are much more …'

> These life-givers and death-wielders are 'queens' or 'ladies' and as such they remained in individual creeds for a very long time in spite of their official dethronement, militarisation, and hybridisation with the Indo-European heavenly brides and wives. The Old European goddesses never became '*déesses dernières*' even in Christian times. … women as heads of clans or queen-priestesses played a central part in Old Europe and Anatolia, as well as Minoan Crete were a gylany. A balanced, non-patriarchal and non-matriarchal social system is reflected by religion, mythologies and folklore, by studies of the social structure of the elements of a matrilineal system in ancient Greece, Etruria, Rome, Crete, the Basque, and other countries of Europe. [*The Language of the Goddess*]

It's obvious that the next question we need to ask ourselves is what happened to the Primal Goddess after the third millennium BC? Did she disappear after the advent of the patriarchal Indo-European migration, or did she survive the dramatic changes? 'Because her main function was to generate life forces, she was flanked by male animals noted for their physical strength – the domesticated dog, the bull, the ram and the he-goat. In her chthonic and frightening aspect she must have been a Mother Terrible, perhaps yearning for human and animal blood, as indicated by her epiphany in the shape of a ferocious dog,' observes Marija Gimbutas in *The Gods & Goddesses of Old Europe: Myths & Cult Images*.

Magdalenian man had been a mighty hunter and, according to *A Study of History*, in the north-west quarter of the Old World, he lost this means of livelihood when the recession of the latest in a succession of glacial ages brought in its wake alarming changes in the regional flora and fauna. Some of his humbler contemporaries to the south and south-east also partly died out; some decamped still further southwards. Some held their ground and made history.

According to Professor Toynbee, agriculture and, to an almost equal extent, the keeping of domestic animals...

which was the normal concomitant of agriculture in the region. These were the essence of Neolithic culture and its greatest enduring legacy to subsequent, whether or not they were higher in terms of spiritual achievement and value. By achieving the agricultural-pastoral revolution, Old Europeans made themselves into active partners of Nature instead of continuing to be parasites on her like their human predecessors. Before the epiphany of higher religion led to the extrication of the religious activities from the secular side of life, all social and cultural activities were religious activities as well. Husbandry, both vegetable and animal, certainly had a religious, as well as an economic, aspect to begin with; and the agricultural-pastoral revolution might never have been achieved if it had not been a religious revolution in one of its aspects.

So ... where do we find the shrines of the Primal Goddess? In answer, they are much closer than we think but it requires the stripping away of the aeons of mistransliteration that have served to cloak the Old European Goddess in mystery. In truth she survived the superimposed Indo-European culture. She was the predecessor of the Hecate-Artemis-Cybele triad and continued to be honoured through the Bronze Age, then through Classical Greece, and even into later history is spite of transformations of her outer form and the many different names that were applied to her.

The Hearth Fire

Excavations of what are thought to be domestic shrines of Old Europe, take the form of rectangular houses divided into two rooms one of which was furnished with an oven, a nearby grindstone and an altar. And at the heart of this social structure, the hearth-oven provided warmth and light, food and protection; it came to symbolise the regenerating, life-giving essence that had been suppressed. The hearth became the central point in every home, the focus for the family and community. On the hearth the spirits of the ancestors were probably honoured and the Goddess invoked; it was where the people prayed and continued to work their magic by the light of the hearth fire. The Fire Element required boundaries so it could be tended and fed as the embers began to dim, because this was the hearth fire, which remained the heart of the home under the convenient cover of domesticity. In contemporary traditional witchcraft the cauldron still symbolises all this – the sacredness of the hearth fire.

Fire is the agent of purification and renewal, and therefore of sacrifice and regeneration; the idea that fire embodies a form of divinity is a basic theme of the world's beliefs. Even in its simplest, most domestic form, fire is an awesome sight; a friendly hearth and a symbol of domesticity and peace. *Man, Myth & Magic* reminds us however, that fire is an elementary force imprisoned within a made-made cage, ready at the least relaxation of vigilance to escape from its prison and reduces homes to ashes. And if we are sensible, this is exactly the same way we should regard the power of the Primal Goddess ... uncontrollable, unstoppable and deadly!

Nevertheless for centuries, the hearth remained such an integral part of a community, usually its central and most important feature, a concept that has been generalised to refer to a home-place or household, in the terms that have come down to us as 'hearth and home' and 'keep the home fires burning'. And there really is something magical about the way a fire lights up a room; sending shadows dancing across the walls, a cosy orange glow from the flames, casting out its warming light and forcing back the chilly darkness as the days grow shorter. Staring into the flickering flames can inspire the imagination and evoke prehistoric fascination as we stare into the glowing embers. And later, to keep the hearth guarded against negative energies, an old iron horseshoe was kept in the bottom of the grate where the ashes fell.

The centre of Greek life – even in Sparta, where the family had been subordinated to the State – was the domestic hearth, also regarded as a sacrificial altar of Hestia, goddess who was called upon for personal security and happiness. It represented the sacred duty of hospitality that guaranteed against sacrilegious ill-treatment of women-guests who had come under the protection of the domestic or public hearth. Hestia's name means 'hearth, fireplace, altar' while her functions show the hearth's continued importance in the social, religious, and political life of Classical Greece. It was essential for warmth, food preparation, and the completion of sacrificial offerings to deities; in the latter, Hestia was the 'customary recipient of a preliminary, usually cheap, sacrifice'. She was also offered the first and last libations of wine at feasts

According to Robert Graves' in *The Greek Myths*, the

archaic white aniconic, symbolic rather than a literally representational image of the Great Goddess and in use throughout the Eastern Mediterranean, who seems to have been represented by a heap of glowing charcoal, kept alive by a covering of white ash, which was the most cosy and economical means of heating in ancient times. It gave out neither smoke nor flame, and formed the natural centre of family or clan gatherings. By placing hemp, barley grains and laurel on the hot ashes of the charcoal mound, it created a simple and effective way of producing narcotic fumes to aid spiritual communication on a higher mystical level.

In Roman belief, the *Lares Familiares* took care of the household, and were worshipped at the hearth, and included on all important household occasions, such as weddings and births. They were associated with the Penates, the guardians of the store-cupboard and both the Lares and the Penates were given portions at all family meals which were then thrown on the fire in the hearth. Nevertheless, in 392AD, the Emperor Theodosius forbade not only the offering of blood sacrifice, but all forms of pagan worship, including private religious rites. No sacrifice in any place or any city was permitted. Privately, no wine or incense was to be offered, no votive candles or burning lamps, no suspended wreaths, either to one's *genius* (the tutelary spirit of a person or place) or to the Lars and Penates (the household gods) on penalty of death.

And yet as history has proved time and time again, it is impossible to legislate belief out of existence and that which is transmitted orally and secretly can be remarkably tenacious. As historian, J Harvey Bloom observes:

In England about the household hearth were gathered many relics of primitive religion. It was the shrine and centre of family life. Therein dwelt the Fire God(!) and to him offerings of ale and cake were nightly made; to her new home the bride brought a portion of fire from her mother's hearth, and had a fire been allowed to die out the result would have been disastrous. In early homes the fire was lighted in the centre, both for convenience and for divine protection; the smoke escaped as best it could. The hearth was always flat, or a large stone or brick work and in later times was flanked by a settle and a salt-box containing the family's supply of salt. [*Folk Lore, Old Customs and Superstition in Shakespeare Land*]

A reference to keeping campfires, lights, etc. at a traveller's home village burning, often while part of the population travels elsewhere, has been a common theme for thousands of years and down through the ages superstitions have grown up from the importance of the hearth fire. This handful of examples in taken from the Encyclopaedia of Superstitions, Folklore, and the Occult Sciences of the World:

If a log rolls off the andirons in the fireplace, it is a sign of a visitor. You should quickly spit on it and make a wish before it hits the hearth, to ensure the one you wished for to come.

If your chimney is not drawing the smoke up the chimney and it was rolling out into the room, it was taken as a sign that a witch is sitting on top of your chimney and you should go outside to shoo her off.

Should you mark the back of the fireplace, you will have bad luck.

When sparks fly out of the fire, a maiden may expect a call from her sweetheart.

Never poke another man's fire unless you've known him for more than seven years. It could provoke all kinds of misunderstandings.

Keeping a fire all the time, without letting it go out is a sign that you will always be well supplied with everything.

The hearth fire then, remains the heart of the home and the symbol of matriarchal power, where women have worked their magic and mysticism since the Old European Goddess was forced into the shadows. The hearth fire is the altar to the Primal Goddess in her regenerative guise since the bread oven was the principal feature of Old European shrines because, according to Professor Gimbutas, the bread prepared in a temple was sacred bread, dedicated to the Goddess and used in her rituals.

Memories of the prehistoric bread-giver linger in some European countries, remembered in processions at harvest time when women gathered flour and baked cakes in her honour. Offerings of bread to the Grain Mother continued to the 20th century in the rural areas of eastern and northern Europe in a practice that can be traced back to Neolithic times.

The Sacred Flame

By contrast, the sacred altar flame is the fire that burns within a temple or sanctuary and forms a bridge between the chthonic realms and the sky, carrying the prayers and entreaties upwards on the perfumed smoke.

At Delphi the white charcoal heap was symbolically translated into limestone for out-doors use, and became the *omphalos*, or navel-boss, frequently shown in Greek vase paintings, which marked the supposed centre of the world. This holy object, which has survived the ruin of the shrine, is inscribed with the name of Mother Earth, stands 11¼ inches high and measures 15½ inches across; and is about the size and shape of a charcoal fire needed to heat a large room. [*The Greek Myths*]

Similarly, numerous triangular or leaf-shaped ladles in stone and clay have been found in Cretan and Mycenaean shrines – some of them showing signs of great heat – and seem to have been used for tending the sacred fire. The charcoal mound was sometimes built on a round, three-legged clay table; examples gave been found in the Peloponnese, Crete and Delos – one of them from a chamber tomb near Knossos, had the charcoal still piled on it.

This was not a structure used to receive a sacrifice, but simply to hold the fire for the purposes of veneration, probably contained within a metal or clay bowl.

The sacred fire of Vesta was a sacred eternal flame in ancient Rome, and tended by the Vestal Virgins who, by analogy, also tended the life and soul of the city through the sacred fire that was renewed every year on the Kalends of March. This sacred fire burned in Vesta's circular temple, built in the Roman Forum below the Palatine Hill in pre-Republican times and among its sacred objects was the Palladium, a statue of Pallas Athena supposedly brought by Aeneas from Troy (Anatolia). The rites of Vesta ended in 394AD by order of Theodosius when the fire was extinguished and the College of Vestals disbanded.

Nevertheless, in even by ancient times the Old European Goddess had been unknowingly incorporated into the Roman religious system. Cybele, for example, was a goddess who may have a possible precursor in the earliest Neolithic at Çatalhöyük, Anatolia, where statues of plump women, (dating to the 6th millennium BC), have been found in excavations. Her Phrygian cult was later adopted and adapted by Greek colonists of Asia Minor and spread to mainland Greece and its more distant western colonies around the 6th century BC. In Greece, Cybele met with a mixed reception and was associated with mountains, town and city walls, fertile nature, and wild animals. In Rome, she was later known as Magna Mater ('Great Mother') and the State adopted and developed a particular form of her cult after the Sibylline oracle recommended her conscription as a key religious ally in Rome's second war against Carthage.

Similarly in Phrygian art of the 8th century BC, the cult attributes of the mother-goddess included attendant lions, a bird of prey, and a small vase for her libations or other offerings. The inscription *Matar Kubileya/Kubeleya* at a Phrygian rock-cut shrine, dated to the first half of the 6th century BC, is usually read as 'Mother of the mountain' and consistent with Cybele as any of several similar tutelary goddesses, each known as 'mother' and associated with specific Anatolian mountains or other localities: a goddess thus 'born from stone', according to Lotte Motz in *Faces of the Goddess*. By the 2nd century AD, the geographer Pausanias attests to a Magnesian (Lydian) cult to 'the mother of the gods', whose image was carved into a rock-spur of Mount Sipylus that believed to be the oldest image of the Goddess. At her shrine at Pessinus in Phrygia, a mother goddess - identified by the Greeks as Cybele - took the form of an unshaped stone of black meteoric iron that was removed to Rome in 294BC. According to Professor David Freedberg:

The sacred stone of Pessinus (the *agalma diipetēs* as it was tellingly called) ... this small and light black meteorite, which was regarded as the Great Mother, was brought to Rome and, encased in silver, was substituted for the mouth (or face) of the statue of Cybele. 'We all see it today,' says Arnobius, 'put in that image instead of a face, rough and unhewn, giving the figure a countenance that is by no means lifelike'. This sacred stone, as many others, was deliberately left unworked because it was in that state that its sacredness resided. Shaping it would presumably have deprived it of its sacred content (or, at least diminished it); the only course left was to have it set in such a way as to emphasize or make plain its divine status.

Images and iconography in funerary contexts, and the ubiquity of her Phrygian name *Matar* ('Mother'), suggest that she was a mediator between the 'boundaries of the known and unknown': the civilized and the wild, the worlds of the living and the dead, suggests Lynn Roller in *In Search of God the Mother: The Cult of Anatolian Cybele*. "Her association with hawks, lions, and the stone of the mountainous landscape of the Anatolian wilderness, seem to characterize her as mother of the land in its untrammelled natural state, with power to rule, moderate or soften its latent ferocity, and to control its potential threats to a settled, civilized life."

Similarly, from the Old European-Minoan culture, we also find Britomartis, who was worshipped as the 'mood-goddess of the mountains' and who represented the female spirit of Nature; she was the Great Goddess of life, death and regeneration. As a 'Mountain Mother' she appeared with Gorgon-like features, and in Minoan art was portrayed with demonic features accompanied by feral animals. Depictions show her holding the double-headed axes of power and her symbols the divine snakes.

Early Crete had an elaborate and wealthy culture and based its worship on the female principle of Nature. When patriarchy overran the island, the theology of this culture was distorted and goddesses demoted to heroines with their legends grafted onto those of the Greek heroes. Britomartis is one who has survived in this manner but some scholars suggest she may well be the greatest goddess of Minoan Crete. She is traditionally depicted as a young, lithe and strong hunter, often carrying arrows; an image that was merged as a spoil of war, with the image of Artemis and has remained as her image to this day.

The ancient people of Etruria (or Etruscans) had developed a complex and dominant culture in Italy and by 650BC, it surpassed other ancient Italic peoples, with an influence seen to extend beyond Etruria's boundaries. Here Uni was the multi-faceted (Old European) Great Goddess who was worshipped from very ancient times by the tribes of central and south-central Italy, as well as by the Etruscans, and later assimilated with Hera. Rome eventually obliterated the entire culture and it is only recently that researchers have begun translating an inscription on an ancient Etruscan stone slab that mentions the powerful deity Uni and suggests the possible existence of an underground cult in the area dedicated to the Goddess some 2,500 years ago.

Another hypothesis gives credence to a claim made by a DNA study, suggesting that the Etruscans were probably an indigenous population, appearing to fall very close to a Neolithic population from Central Europe, with genetic links between Tuscany and Anatolia dating back to at least 5,000 years.

At the far reaches of the Roman Empire, there was a sacred flame burning in Kildare reaching back into pre-Christian times. Scholars suggest that priestesses used to gather on the hill of Kildare to tend their ritual fires while invoking an Old European Goddess named Brigid to protect their herds and to provide a fruitful harvest. When St. Brigid's monastery and church were built in Kildare her 'priestesses' continued the custom of keeping the fire alight; for her nuns the fire represented the new light of Christianity, which in fact, had only reached Irish shores early in the fifth century. When Gerald of Wales (Giraldus Cambrensis) a Welsh chronicler visited Kildare in the twelfth century, he reported that the fire of St Brigid was still burning and that is was being tended by nuns of St Brigid. Some historians record that a few attempts were made to have the fire extinguished but without success; it survived possibly up to the suppression of the monasteries in the sixteenth century.

The sacred flame was re-lit in 1993, in the Market Square, Kildare, and since then, the Brigidine Sisters in Kildare have tended the flame in their centre, *Solas Bhride*. Each year the flame burned in the town square for the duration of *Fcile Bride* and from 1st February 2006, St. Brigid's Day, the flame was perpetually lit in the town square from the flame tended in *Solas Bhride* for the previous fourteen years. Here, in Ireland, and sanctioned by the

Roman Catholic Church, the sacred flame of the Primal Goddess burns anew.

In modern times

A fire pit can vary from a pit dug in the ground to an elaborate gas burning structure of stone, brick, or metal; the common feature being that they are designed to contain fire and prevent it from spreading in the garden. On a more modest level, most of us have a small fire-proof container that we can light to honour our deities in the company of family and friends to celebrate the Old Ways, especially if there's no open fire inside the home. A 'patio heater' or *chiminea* - a freestanding, front-loading fireplace or oven with a bulbous body and a vertical smoke vent or chimney, is an ideal substitute. The first use of a traditionally designed *chiminea* is recorded around 400 years ago but they are remarkably evocative in shape to the prehistoric bread oven illustrated in *The Language of the Goddess*.

And there is always something evocative about the smell of burning wood and leaves in the open with an almost magical smoke filling the air. This smoke has an incredibly rich smell which evokes other times and other places, people, seasons, long days, crisp nights, bare trees, incipient winter, especially if burning apple or cherry wood. The image of the Old European Goddess in her primitive form has all but faded from our racial memory but there will always be those who are aware of her existence. For those who answer the call of Old Craft are taught that called or not called, the god(dess) *will* be present. While fresh flowers, wheat or grasses are placed on the hearth stone ... whenever a handful of incense is thrown into the flames and its smoke rises ... and freshly baked bread is made as an offering and consumed in her name ... she *will* be there.

The Hearth Fire: Exercise 3

Wherever we live in the world, the Hearth Fire remains as sacred at any Temple or Need-Fire and even today many people instinctively insist of having a 'real' fire in their homes without realising that they are following an age-old tradition. It is natural to revere fire, for it is one of the primal elements of nature and magic. It drives away the cold and the wild beasts, cooks food, burns away trash and uncleanness, sheds light in the darkness, serves as a signal to travellers, and brings people together around the hearth in time-honoured fashion of acknowledging the Primal Goddess and all she stands for.

- **The hearth is the domestic altar and in witches' homes it is not uncommon to find a prominent hearth stone adorned with candles and flowers. Robert Herrick's poem, The Spell, would be an ideal ritual cleansing or banishing working for hearth and home.**

Holy water come and bring;
Cast in the salt for seasoning;
Set the brush for sprinkling;
Sacred spittle bring ye hither;
Meal and it now mix together;
And a little oil to either;
Giver the tapers here their light;
Ring the saint's bell, to affright
Far from hence the evil sprite.

If it isn't possible to have an open fire then create a small area with a tile or piece of flat slate where joss sticks or an oil evaporator can be left to burn without fear of conflagration. Look upon this as your own sacred flame of the Primal Goddess.

Chapter Four

Beyond the Veil

Although the concept might be at odds with current thinking, in Old Europe their world was not polarized into male and female as it was among the incoming Indo-European cultures because both principles were manifested side by side. The male divinity in the shape of a virile man or male animal appears to affirm and strengthen the forces of the creative and active female. Neither is subordinate to the other; by complementing one another, their power is doubled.

The last bastion of Old European mythical imagery and religious practices continued in Minoan Crete until it was overrun by the Greeks in c.1450BC. Evidence suggests that the Minoans disappeared so suddenly because of the massive volcanic eruption in the Santorini Islands. We know now that the eruption and the collapse of the volcanic cone into the sea caused tsunamis which devastated the coasts of Crete and other Minoan coastal towns. Perhaps the eruption in 1645 had weakened the Minoans to the point that they were easy targets for the Mycenaeans when they arrived about 200 years later. The survivors of these catastrophes of invasion and natural disasters had to go somewhere, and wherever they went in the New Europe, they knew their goddess had to remain 'hidden' if she were to survive.

Professor Arnold Toynbee maintains that civilisations have always been brought to grief by their own faults and failures, and not by any external agency; but after a society has dealt itself the fatal blow and is on the point of dissolution, it is usually overrun and finally liquidated by barbarians from beyond its frontiers.

The crystallisation of a universal state's frontiers seems to be the crucial event, for this cuts the barbarians off from peaceful social contact and pens them up until the moment comes for their destructive descent. This barbarian pressure builds up, and the barbarians possess an ever-increasing advantage over the embattled civilisation, so that their ultimate victory is inevitable. On the desolated homelands of the former civilisation, the barbarians enjoy a brief 'heroic age' ... and are the brooms which sweep the historical stage clear of the debris of a dead civilisation; this destruction feat is their historic task, and it has been glorified, to the point of becoming almost unrecognisable in their myths and poetry. [*A Study of History*]

We don't know what 'faults and failures' led to the Old European culture being overrun by the Indo-Europeans, but as Professor Gimbutas's concluding comments in *The Gods & Goddesses of Old Europe* point out, the teaching of Western civilisation usually starts with the Greeks and rarely do people ask themselves what forces lay behind those beginnings. "But European civilisation was not created in the space of a few centuries; the roots are deeper – by six thousand years. That is to say, vestiges of the myth and artistic concepts of Old Europe, which endured from the seventh to the fourth millennium BC were transmitted to the Western world and became part of its cultural heritage" ...

Traditional British Old Craft is not generally seen as gender specific but in truth, its beliefs do tend to lean towards the male aspect since the female element of deity remains veiled and a mystery. In other words, the 'God' is the public face of traditional British Old Craft while the 'Goddess' remains in the shadows, revered and shielded by her protector. Not because she is some shy and defenceless creature, but because face to face she would be too terrible to look upon! Or as the scientist who discovered the deadly Marburg filovirus observed when he saw the virus particles: "They were white cobras tangled among themselves, like the hair of Medusa. They were the face of Nature herself, the obscene goddess revealed naked ... breathtakingly beautiful."

One of the original concepts of the 'hidden goddess' can be found in Amunet, the pre-dynastic Egyptian Goddess of Air or Wind, whose name means 'She Who is Hidden', 'The Invisible One' or 'That Which is Concealed'. She was one of eight primeval deities who existed before the beginning of the world but was simply the feminine form of Amun's own name, depicted as a woman wearing the Red Crown of Lower Egypt. Before the First Dynasty she had been assimilated with Neith, whose primary cult in the Old Kingdom was established in Saïs by King HorAha of the First Dynasty, in an effort to placate the residents of Lower Egypt by the ruler of the unified country.

The original imagery of Neith was as deity of the unseen and limitless sky and the Greek philosopher Proclus, who spent time travelling and being initiated into various mystery cults, wrote that the inner sanctum of the temple of Neith in Sais carried the following inscription: *I am the things that are, that will be, and that have been. No one has ever lifted the veil by which I am concealed.*" It is an inscription often attributed to Isis in later times but the true dedication belongs to Neith – the original 'hidden goddess'.

In Greek mythology, it is possible that Persephone was also a 'hidden goddess' since Homer describes her as the 'formidable, venerable majestic princess of the underworld, who carries into effect the curses of men upon the souls of the dead'. Persephone held an ancient role as the dread queen of the Underworld, and it was forbidden to speak her name. This tradition came from her merging with the very old chthonic divinity Despoina (the mistress), whose real name could not be revealed to anyone except those initiated to her Mysteries. Also, Persephone as a vegetation goddess and her mother Demeter were the central figures of the Eleusinian Mysteries that predate the Olympian pantheon; the origins of which are uncertain, but they was based on very old agrarian cults of the rural communities.

Possibly the earliest possible representations are those prehistoric 'Venus' figurines that date from the Upper Palaeolithic period, found from Western Europe to Siberia. These items were carved from soft stone, bone or ivory, or formed of clay and fired. To date over 200 of the figurines have been found – all sharing the same characteristics of pendulous breasts, sagging stomachs and buttocks; the heads are small and featureless, i.e., without identity, but despite the large numbers of figurines discovered, archaeologists are still at a loss to explain the true function of these featureless women. According to anthropologist, Richard Leakey, the figures were assumed to represent a continent-wide female fertility-cult, although 'recent and more critical scrutiny, however, shows a great deal of diversity in the form of these figures, and few scholars would now argue for the fertility-cult idea'.

In reality, almost all Neolithic goddesses are composite images with an accumulation of traits from the pre-agricultural and agricultural eras. Those 'buxom wenches' with their massive thighs, breasts and buttocks that suggest a prehistoric society weaned on junk food, or suffering from thyroid dysfunction were only one aspect of the Goddess. In other sculptures of the time we see lithe, elegant figures of the Cycladic and Stargazer imagery, and the sinuous grace of the engraved rock 'dancers' from the cave of Addaura in Sicily.

Unfortunately there is no explanation for these radical differences only to suggest a change in the meaning and ritual purpose of the images. Nevertheless, they all share a distinctive feature of a strong but featureless face: her image remains hidden because we are *deliberately* prevented from seeing the true face of the Primal Goddess. A concept that was rejuvenated with the replacing of the sculpted face of Cybele with ...

... a certain stone of no great size, which could be carried in a man's hand without exerting any pressure on him, dusky black in colour, uneven with some edges projecting, and which we all see today placed in that very image in lieu of a face, rough and uncut, giving to the image a countenance by no means life-like ... [Arnobius, Case Against the Pagans]

The implication was that the stone still survived in Arnobius's time (250-300AD), assuming he reported accurately that he had seen it, and that it formed only part of a larger image, probably of the goddess herself. In other words, thousands of years later this sacred stone, was deliberately left unworked because it was in that state that its sacredness resided.

In more modern times, however, there are traceable elements of the 'Hidden Goddess' or the 'Divine Feminine' in Freemasonry and the Marian Cult within the Roman Catholic Church. In *Freemasonry and the Hidden Goddess* by William Boyd, the author has assembled a considerable amount of information and illustrations that suggested concealed goddess symbolism within Masonic imagery, despite the fact that it is seen as a male-dominated secret society. He drew a large amount of symbolism from beautiful classical copper-plate etchings, most of which represent the different elements of Freemasonry in female form. In an age when nearly all women were deprived of education, it would possibly have made more sense to represent arts and sciences as old men with beards, which was the usual custom in the past, unless the feminine aspect played an important role behind the scenes.

The Virgin Mary attained cult status in the earliest centuries of the fledgling Christian Church, and despite a concerted effort begun by the Vatican forty years ago to de-emphasise her, the mother of Jesus remains a powerful, albeit polarizing, force within the Catholic Church; although the Church's liberal wing still claims the Marian Cult is an unnecessary anachronism. But why did the early Church feel a need to elevate Mary to a position of worship? Perhaps to help spread Christianity, 'since ancient people needed a feminine figure in their worship", suggests Sarah-Jane Boss in *Empress and Handmaid: On Nature and Gender in the Cult of the Virgin Mary*. "They were used to having goddesses. Moreover, virgin births of gods figured prominently in many ancient myths and pioneering Christians often piggybacked on Paganism to speed conversion."

Surprisingly, despite the torturous methods of the Inquisition, the infamous *Malleus Maleficarum* makes scant mention of any female deity as part of the witch-cult, and yet surely the worship of a principal female deity at that point in history would have been considered a greater, if not equal heresy than paying homage to any Devil? Even Margaret Murray's more sympathetic scrutiny of the witch-trials (*The Witch-Cult in Western Europe*) contains no reference to any 'goddess' connected to witchcraft, except for a passing mention of the decree of the Council of Ancyra, referring to 'certain wicked women ... [who] believe and profess that they ride at night with Diana'. The council dismissed these assertions as products of dreams and officially dismissed them as illusory but they were to resurface in an episcopal statute of Auger de Montfaucon, which says, '*Nulla mulier se nocturnis equitare cum Diana paganorum, vel cum Herodiade seu Bensozia, et in numina multitudinem profiteatur'*.

The introduction of Herodias, originally a biblical figure, in connection with a witch-deity was probably another intentional displacement of pagan identity. Herodias is a name linked to *stregheria*, an ancient form of Italian witchcraft, while Bensozia was 'Bona Socia' – the 'Good Neighbour'. All these terms were titles of the concealed Primal Goddess and euphemisms for her real name, which was obviously never spoken aloud or the Church would certainly have recorded it for posterity. It is curious that the Church up to this point dismissed these nocturnal stories of riding to the Sabbat with the 'witch-goddess' as delusional, and the later accusations of the Canon Episcopi and the *Malleus Maleficarum* were merely regurgitated 'facts' from much earlier texts. In her Introduction to *The Witch-Cult in Western Europe*, Margaret Murray is frank enough to state that it was her choice to 'label this ancient religion the Dianic cult' in the absence of any identifiable generic name. Like the early churchmen and academics, she had taken the image of a compatible pagan goddess with similar attributes and created a 'witch-goddess' from classical Graeco-Roman sources.

Ironically, Shakespeare's three witches called upon Hecate in *Macbeth*, although some claim this as a later addition by Thomas Middleton because the extract contains stage-directions for two songs which have been found in Middleton's *The Witch*, Act V, scene ii: '*Black spirits and white, red spirits and grey, Mingle, mingle, mingle, you that mingle may*' – adaptations that often appear in both traditional witchcraft and contemporary Wicca. There is also evidence that part of this song was drawn from Reginald Scot's 16th-century *Discoverie of Witchcraft*, where Scott refers to 'white spirits and black spirits, gray spirits and red spirits'.

In Charles Leyland's translation of *Aradia: the Gospel of the Witches*, Diana was named as the Tuscan goddess of the witches, whose daughter Aradia (or Herodias) was sent to earth to teach her followers the art of witchcraft and sorcery. Leland's account described an Italian legend of a woman who ... 'travelled far and wide, teaching and preaching the religion of old times, the religion of Diana, the Queen of the Fairies and of the Moon, the goddess of the poor and the oppressed. And the fame of her wisdom and beauty went forth over all the land, and people worshiped her, calling her La Bella Pellegrina (the beautiful pilgrim)'.

The identity of any indigenous British goddesses, however, has been submerged beneath the influx of Romano-Celtic deities and it is extremely difficult to shake loose the tangled skein despite the fact that British Old Craft was a definite belief with customs and observances as highly developed as that of any other faith in the Old World. In *Chances of Death* (1897), Professor

Karl Pearson visualised her as the Mother-Goddess worshipped chiefly by women but Murray claims that it was only on very rare occasions that deity appeared in female form to receive the homage of the followers. For the best part, the goddess remained hidden behind a veil of secrecy and mystery.

Traditionally, in old British witchcraft this elusive goddess is merely referred to as 'Lady' or 'Dame', titles that are also customarily taken by the female leader of the group or coven. This inaccessibility of the Primal Goddess is due to her being, in her primitive form, too terrible to look upon; she is unapproachable simply because to do so, would probably mean certain death to the seeker – if not as a result of *lèse-majesté* then surely from shock.

This is the face of cosmic power that remains veiled to us for all time for our own safety; together with Chaos, she belongs to the first principles of the cosmos and from her were born heaven and the sea. Neither benevolent nor malevolent, the Primal Goddess has little concern for the supplications and obsequiousness of the individual. It's said that humans create their gods in their own image but the Primal Goddess is as far removed from us as the fantasy Facebook images are from our primitive tribal Ancestors. Originating in Old Europe, she is the multifaceted faceless image of the *Matres,* Roman matriarchal divinities, usually represented as a trinity and now over-simplified in the maiden, mother and crone of contemporary paganism.

This Primal Goddess might be seen as the embodiment of Gaia or Mother Nature, but as Meriem Clay-Egerton described her actions:

The planet is shaking itself free, initially to try and eradicate the parasites which are disturbing it ... it is no longer a bright and proud future, but dark and sullen. The Earth realizes that to free herself she must destroy herself and start again with new building bricks. But she can't tell the guilty from the innocent, all will go as they must into infinity; the great pool of Chaos. In the future, if there is any future to come – if this environmental niche has not been blown apart or torn to pieces by the so-called dominant animal species – what would an archaeologist find to say about us? Would he consider homo sapiens to be a worthy holder of the planet? Or would he consider them a noisome evil spreading blight, a parasite upon the planet's surface? In all charity he would see them as a dead end: unable to progress further – totally unable to comprehend what had happened to their world – only fit to be superseded by a newer, more intelligent species ...'

It may seem strange in these days of caring, sharing niceness where everyone wants to get on the witchcraft gravy train, that Old Craft witches pay homage to such a remote, uncaring and disinterested deity. How can we revere this faceless, formless, forbidding divinity that would scarcely raise an eyebrow if some cataclysmic happening wiped out humankind and replaced it with a race of highly developed rats or cockroaches? It's quite simple, as Bob Clay-Egerton explained when he described the Power of the One in pure animistic terms: 'That the One is everything, physical and non-physical, literally everything and therefore incomprehensible to our finite understanding. Being everything, the One is male and female and androgyne – not simply a male entity. All things are created in the image of the One because the One is every part of every thing'. Again, he repeats his wife's view that the One has no specific regard or concern for one species, i.e., humankind, among millions of species on one insignificant minor planet, in an outer arm of a spiral galaxy which is one among millions.

It is not uncommon for newcomers to Coven of the Scales to experience difficulty in dealing with such an abstract way of inter-acting with this Oneness that is both at the same time god/goddess, positive/negative, passive/active, light/dark, night/day. We may also use terms such as 'the Old Lass' and 'the Old Lad' to identify the type of 'witch-power' we are summoning but it is not a photo-shop embodiment of those fantasy 'goddesses' of popular Paganism. And yet ... the Primal Goddess of Old Craft is a tangible power that can be tapped into and channelled for magical, mystical and spiritual reasons. It is the elusive power that is released into us at the moment of Initiation when we come face to face with deity and we probably look on the face of the Primal Goddess for the first and last time.

Nevertheless, we need to understand precisely how the Old European Goddess survived and metamorphosed into the Primal or 'Hidden' Goddess of contemporary witchcraft. If the Indo-Europeans were running true to form, then the Old Europeans would have been enslaved or slaughtered, and the more comely of the survivors gradually merged into the invading culture so as to become indistinguishable from it. And judging from the re-emerging later influences in Western and Northern Europe it's possible that the religious intelligentsia of the time managed to get a head-start on the invaders and fled as this new patriarchal culture roared and pounced its way westward.

Over time the Old European Goddess became assimilated with (but not submerged by) the cultures into which her people merged and married. Possibly identifying with Professor Bryan Sykes's 'Ursula' – the oldest of his ancestral DNA mothers and to whom a substantial proportion, about eleven percent of modern Europeans are connected by a maternal link. And whose roots come from the area assigned by Professor Gimbutas as Old Europe, or the much later 'Jasmine', whose clan were agricultural pioneers from the Near East (Anatolia).

All the mass migration that was taking place during those millennia encompasses almost 10,000 years of human society and in *Facing the Ocean*, Professor of European Archaeology, Barry Cunliffe shows that Celts, Bretons and Galicians had a closer kinship with seafaring neighbours than with their English, French, and Spanish countrymen. At the height of Old European culture, to the far west there was at the same time the emergence of an Atlantic identity in a people who lived on the edge of the world. 'This life-style created a collective consciousness that was, and still is today, specifically Atlantic – an identity that has produced cultures of great inventiveness and works of great beauty and originality.'

In *The Language of the Goddess*, Professor Gimbutas examined the hundreds of thousands of potsherds, i.e. pottery fragments, pieces of broken pot or other earthenware item, that have archaeological significance and are the most frequently found artefacts during an excavation. Potsherds are an invaluable part of the archaeological record because the analysis of ceramic changes recorded in them has become one of the primary techniques used by archaeologists in assigning components and phases to times and a particular culture.

When an ancient settlement was violently conquered the victors would often destroy the buildings by pulling down its walls and totally razing it to the ground by fire. This resulted in great building stones being hurled down onto the ceramic items of everyday use. Most were shattered beyond recognition. Like a forensic investigator the ceramic expert needs to assemble all of the available potsherds and carefully piece them together to reconstruct the original. Where missing pieces create a void, making a modern replacement piece fills the gap and from their style, form and colour assists researchers in identifying the culture extant at that time, provides a date for the stratum level, and adds to the chronological record further information about the buried civilisations slowly being uncovered. [*Archaeology Expert*]

In interpreting this 'language' and with the benefit of hindsight we can follow the guidelines of archaeo-mythology – a field that includes archaeology, comparative mythology and folklore – and chart the cross-cultural journey of the Primal Goddess. As the Old Europeans became 'displaced persons' forced to leave their homeland and travel westwards – and northwards as the Ice Age retreated – they took with them their skills and their knowledge, their art and artefacts, their beliefs and their Goddess (who, as we have seen, eventually evolved into the Greek Athene, Hera, Artemis and Hecate; Roman Minerva and Diana; Anatolian Cybele; Irish Morrigan and Brigit; Baltic Laina and Ragana; Russian Baba Yaga, Basque Mari, and many others) … together with their mitochondrial DNA.

The Primal Goddess is, if nothing else, resilient behind her veil of invisibility. And the main theme of this dynamic, hidden power is the mystery of birth and death and the regeneration of life, not only human but all life on earth and indeed in the whole cosmos …

> Symbols and images cluster around the parthenogenic (self-generating) Goddess and her basic functions as Giver of Life, Wielder of Death, and, not less importantly, as Regeneratrix, and around the Earth Mother, the Fertility Goddess young and old, rising and dying with plant life. She was the single source of all life who took her energy from the springs and wells, from the sun and moon, and moist earth. This symbolic system represents cyclical, not linear, mythical time. In art this is manifested by the signs of dynamic motion: whirling and twisting spiral, winding and coiling snakes, circles, crescents, horns, sprouting seeds and shoots. The snake was a symbol of life energy and regeneration, a most benevolent, not an evil creature. [*The Language of the Goddess*]

The fusion of the imagery of Cybele-Hecate-Artemis by the ancient Greeks forged all the elements of the Primal Goddess of the earth-underworld-sky – the original triple-divinity. Cybele, the ancient Phrygian Mother of the Gods, a primal nature goddess worshipped with unrestrained rites in the mountains of central and western Anatolia. She was also the focus of a mystery cult;

private rites with a chthonic aspect connected to a hero cult and exclusive to those who had undergone initiation. Classical literary sources describe joyous abandonment to the loud, percussive music of tympanon, castanets, clashing cymbals and flutes, and to the frenzied 'Phrygian dancing', perhaps a form of circle-dancing by women, to the roar of 'wise and healing music of the gods'.

Hecate can also be traced as an Anatolian primary, mystery-cult goddess and appears in the Homeric *Hymn to Demeter* and in Hesiod's *Theogony*, where she is promoted strongly as a great goddess. In the post-Christian writings of the *Chaldean Oracles* (2nd – 3rd century AD) she was regarded as having rulership over earth, sea, and sky, as well as a more universal role as Saviour (*Soteira*), Mother of Angels and the Cosmic World Soul. Hecate was described as the consort of Khthonian (Underworld) Hermes in the cults of Thessalian Pherai (Pherae) and Eleusis. Both gods were leaders of the ghosts of the dead, and were associated with the spring-time return of Persephone.

Artemis was one of the most widely venerated of the ancient Greek deities and some scholars believe that the name, and indeed the goddess herself, was originally pre-Greek. Homer refers to her as *Artemis Agrotera, Potnia Theron*: goddess of wild animals and the wilderness. As a lunar goddess, she was sometimes identified with the goddesses Selene and Hecate, although only Selene was regarded as the personification of the moon itself.

And just as had happened in ancient Egypt, as the need for understanding grew, so did the spiritual need for more identifiable forms on which to focus the people's devotions. And we know, the common man's mind dwelt on the concrete, not the abstract and so the gods took on the human identities of myth and legend to satisfy the demands of less scholarly folk. The attributes of the multitude of gods and goddesses subsequently extended to create a whole pantheon of relatives and helpers that remain familiar to us today.

It is, therefore, not surprising that with all these merging, amalgamations and mistransliterations of cultural differences that the Primal Goddess lost her identity and retreated into the shadows; where she was to remain for centuries, although her beliefs survived as an undercurrent in many remote, rural areas. The patriarchal cultures that oppressed the gylanic society of Old Europe, nevertheless absorbed the female elements of belief and transformed them into the wives, mothers, sisters and girlfriends of their own gods. The invaders had enough superstitious fear about them not to suppress entirely the deities of the conquered people but to incorporate the beliefs into their own expanding religion – just as Christianity did in its conversion of pagan Europe. It has also been a long established fact that the gods of the conquered people became the demons of the invaders. Nevertheless, the Old European sacred images were never entirely suppressed because 'these most persistent features in human history were too deeply implanted in the psyche'. They could have only been obliterated with the total extermination of the female population.

Which almost came to pass during the European witch-hunts of the 15-18ᵗʰ centuries, when the Great Regeneratrix – the overseer of cyclic life energy and death – was turned into a witch, or at least her followers were. The Inquisition systematically hanged and/or burned thousands of victims who were mostly simple country women who had learned and preserved the secret lore of the Goddess from their mothers and grandmothers. In 1484, the Pope denounced witchcraft as an organised conspiracy of the Devil's army against the Holy Roman Empire and the witch was a disciple of Satan. In 1486, the handbook of the witch hunters, *Malleus Maleficarum*, appeared and became the indispensable authority for terror and murder. And yet the chief 'accused' in this monstrous and long-running trial of faith was not the Goddess herself, who was never mentioned by the prosecuting counsel!

The Primal Goddess gradually retreated into the depths of forests or into the mountains where she remains to this day – and where those of Old Craft go to seek her out. But the cycles never stopped turning and the language of the Goddess could always be heard in the rippling of the streams, or being whispered on the wind. And yes, the God is still her protector, shielding her from defilement and prying eyes, keeping the veil securely wrapped around her until she is ready to reveal herself to those true seekers.

The Hearth Fire: Exercise 4

The belief in the sacredness of life-giving water and the sources of rivers, springs and wells extends from prehistory to the present day. The sacred well or spring was a pre-Celtic concept firmly established long before Christianity arrived in the British Isles and was so firmly entrenched in the indigenous mind that the Church felt it more provident to adopt the practice rather than attempt to suppress it. As a result the majority of those famous 'holy wells' in existence today were assigned an appropriate saint in order to strip away any pagan associations.

Sacred wells played an important part in the Old Ways. Some were healing wells, because of the medicinal nature of their waters; some were sacred because they were surrounded by trees of a magical kind. Some were revered because they were dark and could be used for scrying. The water itself was also important for washing away ailments and evil, and for renewal. John Fletcher's (1579-1625) poem *The Holy Well* from *The Faithful Shepherdess* opens by reflecting the prevailing customs of the time:

From thy forehead thus I take
These herbs, and charge thee not awake
Till in yonder holy well
Thrice, with powerful magic spell,

Filled with many a baleful word,
Thou hast been dipped. Thus, with my cord
Of blasted hemp, by moonlight twined,
I do thy sleepy body bind ...

These were the customs of the pre-Celtic people of these islands who believed water (rivers, lakes, streams, wells and springs) marked the entrances to Otherworld, although it appears that offerings of weapons or jewellery were usually broken before being cast into the water. Many pagan shrines were associated with springs, wells, lakes and the sea. Since it was believed that water (feminine) gave birth to spirit (masculine) it was therefore connected with the mother, fertility and creation. Without water, it was thought that even the psychic realm would suffer. Oddly enough, superstition tells us that witches are supposed to be unable to cross running water, and yet the old sacred places were most frequently streams or where streams cross underground. [*Old Year, Old Calendar, Old Ways*]

- If you live in close proximity to a well or natural spring show your respect by clearing away the accumulated debris and throwing a silver coin into the water. A keep a small bowl of spring or rain water by the sacred flame on your altar with a single blossom floating on the surface.

Chapter Five

The Owd Lass and the Owd Lad

Although the serpent is a powerful primal image of Old Craft, there are few mentions of snakes in contemporary Craft lore. Nevertheless, the snake represents life-force, 'a seminal symbol, epitome of the worship of life on this earth. It is not the body of the snake that was sacred, but the energy exuded by this spiraling or coiling creature which transcends the boundaries and influences the surrounding world. The snake was something primordial and mysterious, coming from the depths of the waters where life begins'[Language of the Goddess].

There was a widespread belief that snakes as household gods, were guardians of the family and livestock; they assure fertility increase and health. Furthermore the snake was linked to that that of the dead, specially the ancestors of the family, and so the creature symbolises the continuity of life between the generations. The awakening of the snake after winter's sleep meant the awakening of nature and was celebrated all over Europe, and magical healing herbs were in her possession.

Nevertheless there are only three indigenous snakes in the British Isles which is at the northern edge of the range for reptiles. They favour woodland with open areas for basking with areas of close cover nearby for shelter and nests. Open spaces, glades, rides and paths can provide these kinds of habitat in abundance.

- **Adder**, Vipera berus or viper as it sometimes called is the only venomous reptile in the British Isles, but is generally shy and non-aggressive. It can be variable in colour – even black – and has a distinctive diamond shaped or zigzag pattern along their backs. Adders have a vertically slit pupil that gives it its 'devilish' look.

- **Grass snake**, Natrix natrix is non-venomous but it is the largest snake in the British Isles, favouring rough land and pastures, open woodland, wet heathland, gardens, parks and hedgerows and is a good swimmer. The dorsal surface is green or brown with dark bars and a yellow or cream and black neck collar; the ventral surface is white or cream with black markings. Grass snakes have a round pupil.
- **Smooth snake**, Coronella austriaca is non-venomous, secretive and a very rare, due to the destruction of heathland. It is similar to the adder but the dark spots or stripes on the back are not like the well-formed zigzag pattern of the adder. They also have polished scales, are more slender and have a round pupil with a gold iris.
- **Slow worm**, Anguis fragilis although it may look like a small snake, the slow worm is actually a legless lizard. Their beautiful colours vary from brown to grey or bronze; the young have a dark spot on the top of the head and a continuous black stripe along their back.

It is the grass snake, however, that is sacred within Old Craft where they are attributed with powers of wisdom and a cunning nature. Unfortunately much of the folklore has drifted into obscurity but the creature's regular renewal in sloughing off its old skin and hibernating made it a symbol of the continuity of life and a link with Otherworld. Is it any wonder then, that Coven of the Scales took its name from this process of ecdysis when the snake's vision is impaired and its behaviour can become unpredictable and aggressive since the snake is in a vulnerable state. After three to four days, the eyes become clear again and the snake begins seeking out rough surfaces to help complete the process – hence the 'scales falling from the eyes' enabling us to be able to see a situation clearly and accurately. When the scales fall from our eyes, we suddenly know and understand the truth as our mental or spiritual blindness has been removed.

The Old European snake is clearly a benevolent creature, except when the death-wilding aspect of the Goddess is represented. In art we do not find anything that reflects it being evil. This then is the opposite of what is found in Indo-European and [some] Near Eastern mythologies where the serpent symbolizes evil powers. Because the snake is seen as immortal it is a link between the dead and the living; snakes embody the energy of the ancestors and this is possibly why a snakeskin garter is worn by the leader or Dame (and sometimes the Magister) of a traditional Old Craft coven. Usually made from a green grass-snake's skin and in most cases worn above the left knee, the garter is the only piece of formal ritual regalia that signified a medieval witch's rank.

During this period of English history (1154-1485) the Plantagenet's were on the throne and since legend claimed that they were descended from the serpentine sorceress Mélusine, it was hardly likely that they were going to get themselves into a lather over the prospect of accusations of witchcraft, except to use it as a political weapon against one another. Which they did with some frequency ... In fact, so tolerant were the Plantagenet's of witchcraft that claims have been made that the highest Order in the Land – the Order of the Garter – stems from Edward III's quick witted defence of his mistress whose garter fell to the floor while she was dancing with him.

Supposedly the whole room went silent (which assumes that the rest of the Court knew what that particular garter symbolised), and waited to see what the King would do. This was the time when the Inquisition was raging across Europe, though it hadn't yet made it to England. According to the story, the King picked the garter up and tied it to his own leg, saying "*Honi Soit Qui Mal Y Pense*", or "Evil to those who think evil of it". It has been suggested that the garter *was* a badge of membership of a witch-cult and by the King placing the garter on his own leg he effectively silenced the nobles and clergy who would have denounced the Countess of Salisbury of being a witch.

According to *Malleus Satani: The Hammer of Satan*, upon further examination the legend is not quite as preposterous as one might first think. Plantagenet ladies were not the shrinking violets that medieval ballads made them out to be and it would take considerably more than a falling garter to raise blush. Historian Thomas Beaumont James even commented that only at the instigation of a king as powerful as Edward III could such a famous Order of chivalry have as its symbol an article of ladies' underwear! So the Countess of Salisbury's garter must indeed have conveyed some significant message to the onlookers.

Generally speaking, Old Craft witches prefer not to associate their deities with any mythology – home-grown or foreign import – instead we refer to them obliquely as the Old Ones, the Owd Lad and Owd Lass, the Lord and Lady, or just Him and Her. Similarly, the Owd Lass doesn't have any tangible form and like the 'light black meteorite, which was regarded as the Great Mother' in ancient times, we consider that the world of Nature in its unworked form is the state in which her sacredness resides. Re-shaping it into a recognisable or more pleasing aspect would deprive the Goddess of her sacredness (or, at least diminish it) and the only course left is to have it set in our minds in such a way as to emphasise or make plain her divine status against the raw framework of the forests and mountains.

The Creator is everything, physical and non-physical, literally everything and therefore incomprehensible to our finite understanding. Being everything, the Creator is male and female and neuter - not just a male energy. All things are created in the image of the Creator, because the Creator is every part of every thing. ... *The Book of Frater Asmodaeus,* A R Clay-Egerton.

The Owd Lass

The reason for the great number and variety of Old European 'goddess' images lies in the fact that this symbolism is lunar and chthonic, celestial and terrestrial, built around the understanding that life on earth is in eternal transformation, in constant and rhythmic change between creation and destruction, birth and death. Therefore, the Primal Goddess is seen in everything and from the earliest of times has been associated with a variety of creatures in a host of manifestations.

Evidence of the Primal Goddess's mysterious ties with the deer and bear can be found in pre-historic times and has been preserved in Scottish and Irish fairytales in which women could shape-shift into deer. Deer portrayals or sculptures of seated women with deer antlers are recorded throughout the Bronze Age and continued into the Iron Age, while stag dances were performed around the New Year in England, Romania and Germany. The Abbots Bromley Horn Dance, recorded as being performed at the Barthelmy Fair in August 1226, is one of the few ritual rural customs to survive the passage of time.

Although bears became extinct in the British Isles about a thousand years ago its symbolic use in heraldry is very old, such as the 'Bear and Ragged Staff' whose origins are lost in the distant past, but have been associated with the Earls of Warwick sine the 14th century. The holiness of the bear, as an animal of great strength and majesty, and the glory of the forest is universal in the northern hemisphere. The other aspect of the bear's holiness, specially related to the female is her association with mother hood. Folk memories tell us that the bear was an ancestress, a mother life-giver; while bear-madonnas in the form of a woman wearing a bear-mask and holding a cub are known from Vinca art of the 5th millennium.

In traditional British Old Craft the embodiment of the Primal Goddess lies in the hare. When the Romans invaded the British Isles, Julius Caesar made the observation that the indigenous people did not regard it lawful to eat the hare. In Ireland the animal's association with women from the Otherworld who could shape-shift into the form of a hare also made eating them taboo. The hare has also featured in the mythology of other cultures for thousands of years, including being associated with the Northern European Saxon Goddess Ēostre.

Carbon dating of fossils show hares were present in Ireland as far back as 28000BC. In Irish folklore the hare is also often associated with the Otherworld (*Aos Si*) community whose world was reached through mists, hills, lakes, ponds, wetland areas, caves, ancient burial sites, cairns and mounds. Those entities were seen as very powerful and the hare's link to them sent a warning that any who harm the animal could suffer dreadful consequences. Shape-shifters were often said to take the form of the hare. This solitary creature was admired for strength, speed; was noted for being active at night and associated with the moon. They were seen as mysterious and magical, and so thought of as an animal to be treated with respect.

A study in 2004 followed the history and migration of a symbolic image of three hares with conjoined ears. In this image, three hares are seen chasing each other in a circle with their heads near its centre and while each of the animals appears to have two ears, only three ears are depicted. The ears form a triangle at the centre of the circle and each is shared by two of the hares. The image has been traced from rural churches in the English right back along the Silk Road to China, via western and eastern Europe and the Middle East. The earliest occurrences appear to be in cave temples in China, dated to the Sui dynasty (6th to 7th centuries) ... and has been adopted as the modern emblem of Coven of the Scales.

Dogs, and particularly hounds, also feature heavily in British folklore, echoing the Old European associations as companions to the Goddess – which may also explain why the incoming Abrahamic religions considered them to be unclean, i.e. pagan.

Dogs were also common sacrificial animals in antiquity and certainly no creature deemed to be unclean would have been fit as an offering for divinity. Witches were often said to be able to shape-shift into a dog, and old woodcuts show dogs to have been considered familiars that could be sent out to bewitch or torment their enemies. And since the British are known dog-lovers, many of these fortunate creatures are elevated to a god-like status, with the Coven stepping over them if they choose to occupy floor-space within the Circle!

It's been said that the Celts came to Britain specifically for the black bee and its honey. Even the Welsh bards of old called Britain the 'Isle of Honey' due to the sheer number of wild bees flying to and fro. In Celtic myth, bees were regarded as having great wisdom and acted as messengers between worlds, able to travel to the Otherworld, bringing back messages from the gods. In the western isles of Scotland, bees were thought to embody the ancient knowledge of the druids. This led to the Scottish lore of the secret knowledge of the bees, along with the Scots saying 'ask the wild bee for what the druid knew'. Highlanders believed that during sleep or while in a trance, a person's soul left the body in the form of a bee.

It is still necessary to treat bees as members of the family. They should be informed of all family happenings, from births to deaths and events in between, especially weddings. Beekeepers also needed calm voices, as the bees did not take harsh words lightly. Either offense could result in the hives not producing honey ... all the way to leaving their beekeeper. Their leaving was considered very dangerous, as owners who lost their bees were surely doomed to die! The Irish goddess Brigid held bees to be sacred, with her hives bringing their magical nectar from her Otherworld apple orchard.

Toad and frogs occupy a prominent place in the magical folklore of many societies, ancient and modern; some of the earliest representations being found in Old European and ancient Egyptian art. More commonly known from the time of the witch-hunts as witches' familiars, these creatures were, in fact, recognised as being archaic symbols of the Primal Goddess and their appearance in the home was a sign of good fortune. Toads in particular were also associated with the legendary 'horse whisperers' and often kept in rural pantries to keep down invading insects – hence the possible association with familiars. A toad is capable of eating hundreds of insects at one meal and was often kept as pets to clean up cottage pantries infested with ants; their residence in Victorian greenhouses helped to keep this practice alive. Today they can be encouraged to remain in the garden by providing a suitable spot, so they deal with unwanted garden pests. [*A Witch's Treasury of the Countryside*]

Birds, particularly *Corvids* and owls are viewed as messengers between the worlds. Considering that the crow family is said to be the most intelligent species in the bird world, humankind has a long and chequered past with them. They have been feared as symbols of death, revered as creators of the world and worshiped as trickster gods, *because* of their baffling intelligence. Both crows and ravens have appeared in a number of different mythologies throughout the ages. In some cases, they are considered an omen of bad tidings, but in others – particularly in Old Craft - they represent a message from Otherworld. Owls also feature prominently in the myths and legends of a variety of cultures. These mysterious creatures are known far and wide as symbols of wisdom, omens of death, and bringers of prophecy. In some countries, they are seen as good and wise, in others they are a sign of evil and doom to come. There are numerous species of owls, and each seems to have its own legends and lore. In Old Craft they are also considered as messengers from Otherworld.

In addition to forests, caverns and mountains being the triple habitat of the Owd Lass, we should not overlook the importance of certain megalithic sites of western Europe. Folk stories often associate megalithic tombs with a fearsome guardian and some of the cairns are said to be composed from the stones dropped from the apron of the Old Hag. At least forty chambered tombs in Ireland are nicknamed 'Dermot and Grannia's bed', because a young man and his girl, who were eloping, were supposed to have made a bed of stones every night as they fled. But Grannia's name suggests deeper roots than the story itself – the original meaning of *gráinne* is 'ugliness' and this Grannia is the Old Hag of Celtic myth. The other meaning of *gráinne* is grain, which suggests association with regeneration, winter and death. Human death was often likened to Nature's death in winter, when the sun's power is weakest, the days are short and the nights are long.

Neither is it surprising to discover that many western European tomb-shrines have been constructed so that the entrances align with the Winter Solstice since these tombs were said to be entrances to Otherworld … One such tomb, for example, is 6,000-years old and regarded as being similar to megalithic tombs found in Brittany, France; here, however, the entrance passage faces north-west in line with the mid-summer sunset and the stones are dotted with small, salmon-pink stones, freckled with bits of quartz.

It may seem incongruous that Old Craft witches pay homage to such a cold and uncaring deity but by honouring (and caring for) the Primal Goddess's creatures and habitats, we are honouring the Owd Lass in all her guises. There doesn't need to be any special temple with complicated rituals simply because she has no specific regard or concern for one species – humankind, the most dangerous animal of them all - among the millions of species on this insignificant minor planet.

She manifests the natural energies that we use in our pursuit of magical and spiritual progress *and that is the extent of her bounty*. The way in which we choose to develop this desire for knowledge, wisdom and understanding is our own responsibility and, should we decide to follow a path of corruption – in both literal and metaphorical terms – then that too, remains our personal responsibility. There is no redemption or forgiveness in the heart of this Primal Goddess, whose abode is the dark forest, the deep cavern and high mountain peak.

Nevertheless, for Old Crafters the Primal Goddess remains a sigil and symbol, allegory and metaphor, and we learn how to follow her by respecting the world she has created. She is Creatrix, Death-Wielder and Regeneratrix – the eternal triple deity. And the reason we say she is too terrible to look upon is due to the realisation that in her eyes, our lives are worth no more than that of an ant or hover-fly. And, as and when we meet her face to face, it is with the understanding that she is *not* the benevolent Mother-figure of popular paganism; she is a disinterested but not dysfunctional being whom we approach with awe and reverence

The Owd Lad

By contrast, the God is the one who holds our hand in the darkest and remotest of places, and just as he is the protector and champion of his hidden consort, so he offers us his shield in times of need. In recent decades the Owd Lad had taken a bit of a battering in revenge for what Professor Gimbutas describes as 'that aggressive male invasion' but he *was and still is*, an essential opposite of the Primal Goddess in Old European culture, generally accompanying her in the form of a bull, he-goat or ram.

Male figures in Upper Paleolithic art are known from engravings and paintings, but not from sculpture and most of them are fantastic composite beings arising from the imaginative pairing of man and some kind of horned animal. The most interesting and well-known in archaeological literature are the two bison-men and the so-called 'sorcerer' with stag antlers from the cave of Les Trois Fèrers in France. One of them has a bison's head with large horns and a hairy pelt; he is walking or dancing upright on human legs. The 'sorcerer' or shamanic figure was painted separately, four metres from the floor and above an opening in the vicinity of a small rotunda ending in a well.

Nevertheless, whenever the Old European male god's principal epiphany took place it was in the form of a bull, while representations of a bull, he-goat or ram often appear on small ritual vessels. These horned heads embodying virile forces could have played their part in festivals, or in the worship of both the male and the female divinity, which was so prominently displayed in the Minoan culture.

Bulls (or aurochs) were incarnated with the generative force of the Primal Goddess and from late Palaeolithic times to the end of antiquity the bull is always honored as a divine creature, as the manifestation of a god, or as the witness of a god's presence. As Michael Rice points out in *The Power of the Bull*, for more than 15,000 years 'this creature has seized the god-making imagination of men throughout the great band of territory which sweeps from the Atlantic to the borders of India, and south into Africa.

> There is also the compelling sub-plot of the mysterious union of bull and man; even the Minotaur, one of the archetypes of the monster whose nature is as melancholy as it is threatening, has an antiquity, which reaches far back into our kind's more distant past ... The bull leads his followers into some very dark caverns; literally so since the bull is a chthonic creature and is, however mysteriously, associated with the forces which are found under the earth. The bull is identified with earthquake, with the roar of volcanoes and landslip, and with flood. The gods who assume its form are as often the gods of the underworld ...

In this form the bull gives us the Triple God of the earth, the underworld ... and the stars, because the bull is also a celestial creature of magic and divination. Throughout antiquity the bull was identified with a particular group of constellations that can be traced at least to the third millennium BC, and probably much earlier still to that mysterious 'Hidden God' – Asterion – 'ruler of the stars' who lies at the heart of the Cretan labyrinth and offers a completely different explanation of the symbolism than the later Greek myth of the fearsome Minotaur.

Completing the 'horned' aspect of the Primal Goddess's companion male animals, we find that while sheep are generally docile, non-aggressive animals, this is not usually the case with rams, especially during the breeding season. Rams can be very aggressive and have been known to cause serious injuries, even death, to people. A ram should never be trusted, even if it is friendly or was raised as a pet. On the other hand, goats of both sexes symbolize fertility, vitality and ceaseless energy. The male is the epitome of masculine virility and creative energy, while the female typifies the feminine and generative power and abundance – a quality that was not wasted on the Church fathers when they wanted to create a villain of the piece.

Strangely enough, in Coven of the Scales schooling, Meriem Clay-Egerton always saw Pan as the Horned God ... and the Horned God as Pan. This was a traditional British Old Craft coven that honoured Aegocerus the 'goat-horned' – an epithet of the Greek Pan – not Cernunnos, the stag-horned deity the Celts had brought with them from northern Europe. It should also be understood that although Coven of the Scales held firmly to the philosophy and opinion that all faiths were One and all Paths led to the same Goal, it did not advocate what is now referred to as 'eclectic paganism'. So how on earth could this most ancient of ancient, pre-Olympian Greek deities find his way into the beliefs of traditional witchcraft in Britain?

As we've seen from the work of Professors Cunliffe, Gimbutas and Sykes there have been mass-migrations all over Europe involving people from different regions and cultures since the last Ice Age. Some were invaders, others fleeing from oppression ... and with them they brought their beliefs and customs that eventually merged with those of the people who gave them shelter. Again, the mistransliteration of the worship of the ram and goat-cults of the ancient world played its part.

> The imported imagery of the witches' Horned God (usually Pan or satyr-like) appeared in wood-cuts and engravings in an attempt to terrify the uneducated through the medium of 'pamphlet literature'. Georg Luck, a classicist known for his studies of magical beliefs and practices in the Classical world, stated that the Horned God may have appeared in late antiquity, stemming from the merging of Cernunnos, the antlered god of the Continental Celts, with the Greco-Roman Pan/Faunus, 'a combination of gods which created a new deity, around which the remaining pagans, those refusing to convert to Christianity, rallied and that this deity provided the prototype for later Christian conceptions of the devil, and his worshippers were cast by the Church as witches. [*Pan: Dark Lord of the Forest and Horned God of the Witches*]

Esoterically, Pan, the goat-foot god, is considered to be one of the oldest of the Greek deities and over the ages, has been a symbol of the force of Nature. Like other gods of ancient Greece, Pan also embodies many of the qualities of the world over which he ruled. He is depicted as energetic, sometimes frightening, with the wild, unbridled creative force of Nature that certainly makes him an interesting, and often entertaining, character.

And yet if we hark back to the Old World we find another surprising reference: according to Demosthenes, Pan was a 'natural companion' for Cybele, and there is evidence of their joint cults, with a Pan and woman figure in the Acropolis Museum, Athens. While in *Pindar's Maiden Songs Fragment 95* Greek lyric 5th century BC we find: '*O Pan, that rulest over*

Arkadia, and art the warder of holy shrines . . . thou companion of the Megale Mater (Great Mother) ...' and again in *Pythian Ode 3:* *'But now I wish to voice a prayer to the Meter, the revered goddess to whom, and to great Pan young maids before my door [in Thebes] at nightfall often sing their praise.'* Here in his earliest appearance in literature, Pindar's Pythian Ode iii. 78, Pan is associated with a mother goddess, perhaps Rhea or Cybele and refers to virgins worshipping Cybele and Pan near the poet's house in Boeotia. Pan, of course, is famous for his unfettered sexuality and myth tells us that he enticed the moon goddess by wrapping himself in a sheepskin to hide his 'hairy black goat form', and drew Selene down from the sky into the forest where he seduced her.

In the past fifty-years, the Owd Lad has been almost obliterated from contemporary paganism simply because all his 'roaring and pouncing' is out of sync with social mores of the 21st century – in other words, he makes the women nervous! And as Bryan Sykes observes in *Adam's Curse*: 'It is a weary lament to lay most acts of violence and aggression, from the strictly local to the truly global, squarely at the feet of men. Yet the association is strong and undeniable ...'

And yet ... the Owd Lad *is* the Lady's champion, her knight in shining armour, her protector and defender. He raises her on a pedestal and keeps her from those who would violate her person either by violence or profanity even though the top of the plinth remains empty of female form. He maintains his vigilance in the forest and on the mountain slopes by instilling panic in those who would invade her sanctuary: that sudden sensation of fear, which is so strong as to dominate or prevent reason and logical thinking, replacing it with overwhelming feelings of anxiety and frantic agitation consistent with an animalistic fight-or-flight reaction.

Needless to say, the word derives from antiquity and is a tribute to this most ancient of gods – Pan Pangenetor = 'all-Begetter' and Panphage, 'all-Devourer' - both the giver and the taker of life, and the masculine generative power. He was the god of remote and rugged places, of mountain slopes, woods and forests. The Greeks believed that he often wandered peacefully through the woods, playing a pipe, but when accidentally awakened from his noontime nap he could give a great shout that would cause flocks to stampede. From this aspect of Pan's nature Greek authors derived the word *panikon*, 'sudden fear', the ultimate source of the English word: 'panic' and it may also mean that we've inadvertently stumbled too close to the Primal Goddess's lair if we're suddenly stricken with an inexplicable terror in a lonely place.

From the Old Craft magical perspective, the Owd Lad in the shape of a virile man or male animal affirms and strengthens the forces of the creative and active female. For the purpose of Craft technique, it is also important to understand the energies associated with the male/female aspects of magic. The female-goddess energy within Nature is just as red in tooth and claw as male-god energy – both are equally as merciless as the other. It is also important to understand that this energy (whether male or female) is neither malevolent not benevolent, it is merely *natural energy* waiting to be harnessed for use in Craft magic.

The sexual dynamic within Old Craft has little to do with sex and everything to do with equilibrium when it comes down to natural energy and the law of opposites. It has become the custom in recent years to regard the sole 'balancing' energy as the feminine principle. Equilibrium is a state in which opposing forces or actions are balanced so that one is not stronger or greater than the other; a condition in which all influences cancel each other, so that a static or balanced situation results. Whatever the books may tell us, this is *not* the true *magical* meaning of equilibrium - because magic needs a *catalyst* to create action – something to tip the balance. But it may go a long way in explaining why a large amount of contemporary paganism have been taken over by a form of ritualised religion, as opposed to genuine magical application.

Our exploration of the magical laws of the Universe began with the law of opposites (the principle of polarity). Everything that exists has its opposite: male/female, night/day, water/fire, earth/air, active/passive because this is how the Universe is designed, to grow and expand through contrast and to allow all experiences to be made manifest. Magically speaking, there are times when a working with require active male god-energy during which the female remains passive; on other occasions the female goddess-energy takes the active role while the male remains passive. It is the cause/reason for the spell that provides the catalyst that drives the spell home. Using this technique, neither is subordinate to the other; by complementing one another, their power is doubled.

This intentional use of older and obsolete cultural symbolism, with its total disregard for contemporary social customs may be regarded as anachronistic within 21st century Paganism, since it is a way of thought that belongs to another era and is conspicuously old-fashioned.

And yet ...although misplaced in time, the Primal Goddess of Old Europe needs to be re-discovered in her original setting so that we begin to understand the language, customs and attitudes of the people over which she ruled at the dawn of history and help a contemporary seeker to engage more readily with that period of her reign. Or she will continue to remain a 'hidden' Goddess and out of our reach.

The Hearth Fire: Exercise 5

Within an Old Craft coven, we also find a structure in which the sexes are more or less on equal footing, and where they are linked rather than hierarchically 'ranked'. In keeping with this way of thinking, this title has been produced to act as a companion volume to *Pan: Dark Lord of the Forest & Horned God of the Witches*.

Prayer to the Goddess

An English herbal of the 12th century (MS in the British Museum) and cited by Robert Graves includes a prayer to the Goddess. The prayer addresses the deity with the words:

> *Divine Goddess Mother Nature, who generatest all things and brings forth anew the sun which thou hast given to the nations; Guardian of sky and sea and of all Gods and powers; through thy influence all nature is hushed and sinks to sleep ... Again when it pleases thee, thou sendest forth the glad daylight and nurturest life with thine eternal surety; and when the spirit of man passes, to thee it returns. Thou indeed art rightly named Great Mother of the Gods ...*

...because called or not called, the goddess *will* be present.

Afterthought

In the light of all the new DNA and archaeo-mythological research, Jung's archetypes as primordial images don't seem so ludicrous now, and the similarity of the motifs and themes in myths and symbols of different (European) cultures are more likely to be the results of cross-cultural migrations than proof of the existence of a collective unconscious shared by all human beings. New research has also demonstrated that Neolithic Europe wasn't half as insular as historians has previously led us to believe

Arnold Joseph Toynbee was a British historian, philosopher of history, research professor of international history at the London School of Economics and the University of London, who also maintained in *A Study of History*, that civilisations have always been brought to grief by their own faults and failures, and not by any external agency; but after a society had dealt itself the fatal blow and was on the point of dissolution, it was usually overrun and finally liquidated by barbarians from beyond its frontiers.

In a large number of cultures, societies, and religions, there is some myth or racial memory of a distant past when humans lived together in a primitive and simple state, but at the same time one of perfect happiness and fulfilment. In those days, the various myths assure us, there was an instinctive harmony between humans and Nature. People's needs were few and their desires limited and, as a result, there were no motives for war or oppression. Humans were simple souls and felt themselves close to their gods. These mythical or religious archetypes are inscribed in many cultures, and resurge with special vitality when people are in difficult and critical times.

When Plato wrote about Atlantis in his *Timaeus* and the incomplete *Critias,* he was in old age and was also living through 'disillusioning times'. In short, he was trying to come up with a universal philosophy for 'an ideal state in a far from perfect world', but first he had to grab the contemporary world's attention, and force it back from the brink of the chaos into which it was about to descend, by using shock tactics. The story tells of divine wrath against the luckless Atlanteans for their 'greedy pursuit of wealth and power for its own sake, and to the loss of their own virtue' and a whole range of ancient authors regarded Atlantis as a pure form of allegory ... which is exactly what Plato had intended.

Modern archaeology has since revealed evidence of the destruction of a particular Minoan community on Santorini (the Greek name was Thera), when the volcano erupted and the whole island disappeared beneath the waves. The additional collapse of Cretan culture, at much the same time, no doubt also played its part in the creation of the Atlantis myth and the 'detailed' plan of Atlantis with its inner and outer cities and harbour, bears more than a passing resemblance to a passage in the *Odyssey* ... and Plato would have known his Homer!

Although many of Professor Gimbutas's conclusions have been hotly contested by some of her fellow archaeologists, there appears to be a general agreement that the Old European culture came to an end around 3,500BC at a time when the Indo-European migrations were moving westwards, followed later by the Indo-Aryans. Was this disintegration due to the fact that this peace-loving, matrilineal society was unable to defend itself from its more aggressive, covetous neighbours? Whatever happened, this pre-historic Utopia fell victim to the military resources of its invaders who were more organised for waging war; just as these aggressors themselves eventually fell victim to other newly emerging warrior-cultures.

The Primal Goddess has seen her hearth-fires extinguished and her sacred flames cease to burn - but her power remains as a shining beacon in the darkest forests, the deepest caverns and the highest mountains. For in the remote rural areas where wars and persecutions often pass the people by, her worship has endured in the guise of a variety of different names and personas. She evolved into the Greek Athene, Hera, Artemis and Hecate; Roman Minerva and Diana; Anatolian Cybele and Hecate; Irish Morrigan and Brigit; Baltic Laina and Ragana; Russian Baba Yaga, Basque Mari, and even the Virgin Mary ...

But how do we feel when we suddenly discover that the Great Mother of contemporary Paganism bears no similarity to the primal Great Mother of the Old European world? And what if there *was* a 'magico-spiritual' gene that could be traced back to those distant ancestors who actually worshipped the forebears of the various deities to whom we claim allegiance today? Because there *are* time-honoured things about us all as *individuals* that are bred deep in the bone; we are what our roots (DNA) claim us to be. We cannot escape those ancient racial memories of where we originally came from even if the descendants of yesterday's pagans are now scattered all over the globe.

So ... at what stage in our genetic memory is that factory-installed esoteric 'chip' ready to be activated by those 'complex abilities and the actual sophisticated knowledge', inherited along with other more typical and commonly accepted physical and behavioural characteristics'? What causes us to suddenly 'log-on' to that collective subconscious and become imbued with such a certainty that we can say to ourselves - *"I don't need to believe, I know!"*

Sources & Bibliography

Adam's Curse, Bryan Sykes (Corgi)

The Archetypal Female in Mythology and Religion: The Anima and the Mother of the Earth and Sky, Dr. Joan Relke

Blood of the Isles, Bryan Sykes (Corgi)

A Dictionary of English Surnames, P H Reaney (OUP)

Faces of the Goddess, Lotte Motz (OUP)

Facing the Ocean, Brian Cunliffe (OUP)

Folk Lore, Old Customs and Superstition in Shakespeare Land, J Harvey Bloom (EP Publishing)

The Goddess & Gods of Old Europe, Marija Gimbutas (UCP)

The Greek Myths, Robert Graves (Penguin)

The Iconography and Social Structure of Old Europe: The Archaeomythological Research of Marija Gimbutas, Joan Marler

In Search of God the Mother: The Cult of Anatolian Cybele, Lynn E Roller (UCP)

The Language of the Goddess, Marija Gimbutas (Harper & Row)

The Leaping Hare, John Ewart Evans (Faber)

A Natural History of Man in Britain, H J Fleure and M Davies (Fontana)

Old Year, Old Calendar, Old Ways, Méusine Draco (Ignotus)

Phases in the Religion of Ancient Rome, Cyril Bailey (OUP)

The Power of the Bull, Michael Rice (Routledge)

The Power of Images, David Freedberg (Chicago)

The Seven Daughters of Eve, Bryan Sykes (Corgi)

Starchild I & II, Mélusine Draco (Ignotus)

Traditional Witchcraft & the Pagan Revival, Mélusine Draco (Moon Books)

The Tribes of Britain, David Miles (W&N)

Academic Papers:

http://www.second-congress-matriarchal-studies.com/marler.

html

The Iconography and Social Structure of Old Europe: The Archaeomythological Research of Marija Gimbutas, Joan Marler

https://ejop.psychopen.eu/article/view/401/html

https://ejop.psychopen.eu/article/view/389/html

The Archetypal Female in Mythology and Religion: The Anima and the Mother of the Earth and Sky, Parts I and II Dr. Joan Relke

http://adsabs.harvard.edu/full/2005JIMO...33..135M

Meteor Beliefs Project: Meteor Worship in the Greek and Roman Worlds, A McBeath and A D Gheorghe

https://reconstructingthelabyrinth.wordpress.com/2013/01/03/ asterion-the-starry-minotaur-2/

http://www.theoi.com/Cult/KybeleCult.html

MOON
BOOKS

PAGANISM & SHAMANISM

What is Paganism? A religion, a spirituality, an alternative
belief system, nature worship? You can find support for all these
definitions (and many more) in dictionaries, encyclopaedias, and
text books of religion, but subscribe to any one and the truth will
evade you. Above all Paganism is a creative pursuit, an encounter
with reality, an exploration of meaning and an expression of the
soul. Druids, Heathens, Wiccans and others, all contribute their
insights and literary riches to the Pagan tradition. Moon Books
invites you to begin or to deepen your own encounter, right here,
right now.
If you have enjoyed this book, why not tell other readers by
posting a review on your preferred book site.

Recent bestsellers from Moon Books are:

Journey to the Dark Goddess
How to Return to Your Soul
Jane Meredith
Discover the powerful secrets of the Dark Goddess and
transform your depression, grief and pain into healing
and integration.
Paperback: 978-1-84694-677-6 ebook: 978-1-78099-223-5

Shamanic Reiki
Expanded Ways of Working with Universal Life Force Energy
Llyn Roberts, Robert Levy
Shamanism and Reiki are each powerful ways of healing; together,
their power multiplies. *Shamanic Reiki* introduces techniques to
help healers and Reiki practitioners tap ancient healing wisdom.
Paperback: 978-1-84694-037-8 ebook: 978-1-84694-650-9

Pagan Portals – The Awen Alone
Walking the Path of the Solitary Druid
Joanna van der Hoeven
An introductory guide for the solitary Druid, *The Awen Alone* will
accompany you as you explore, and seek out your own place
within the natural world.
Paperback: 978-1-78279-547-6 ebook: 978-1-78279-546-9

A Kitchen Witch's World of Magical Herbs & Plants
Rachel Patterson
A journey into the magical world of herbs and plants, filled with
magical uses, folklore, history and practical magic. By popular
writer, blogger and kitchen witch, Tansy Firedragon.
Paperback: 978-1-78279-621-3 ebook: 978-1-78279-620-6

Medicine for the Soul
The Complete Book of Shamanic Healing
Ross Heaven
All you will ever need to know about shamanic healing and how to
become your own shaman…
Paperback: 978-1-78099-419-2 ebook: 978-1-78099-420-8

Shaman Pathways – The Druid Shaman
Exploring the Celtic Otherworld
Danu Forest
A practical guide to Celtic shamanism with exercises and
techniques as well as traditional lore for exploring the Celtic
Otherworld.
Paperback: 978-1-78099-615-8 ebook: 978-1-78099-616-5

Traditional Witchcraft for the Woods and Forests
A Witch's Guide to the Woodland with Guided Meditations and
Pathworking
Mélusine Draco
A Witch's guide to walking alone in the woods, with guided
meditations and pathworking.
Paperback: 978-1-84694-803-9 ebook: 978-1-84694-804-6

Wild Earth, Wild Soul
A Manual for an Ecstatic Culture
Bill Pfeiffer
Imagine a nature-based culture so alive and so connected,
spreading like wildfire. This book is the first flame…
Paperback: 978-1-78099-187-0 ebook: 978-1-78099-188-7

Naming the Goddess
Trevor Greenfield
Naming the Goddess is written by over eighty adherents and
scholars of Goddess and Goddess Spirituality.
Paperback: 978-1-78279-476-9 ebook: 978-1-78279-475-2

Shapeshifting into Higher Consciousness
Heal and Transform Yourself and Our World with Ancient
Shamanic and Modern Methods
Llyn Roberts
Ancient and modern methods that you can use every day to
transform yourself and make a positive difference in the world.
Paperback: 978-1-84694-843-5 ebook: 978-1-84694-844-2

Readers of ebooks can buy or view any of these bestsellers by
clicking on the live link in the title. Most titles are published in
paperback and as an ebook. Paperbacks are available in traditional
bookshops. Both print and ebook formats are available online.

Find more titles and sign up to our readers' newsletter at
http://www.johnhuntpublishing.com/paganism
Follow us on Facebook at https://www.facebook.com/MoonBooks
and Twitter at https://twitter.com/MoonBooksJHP